THE SOVIET GULAG

Russian Shorts

Russian Shorts is a series of thought-provoking books published in a slim format. The Shorts books examine key concepts, personalities, and moments in Russian historical and cultural studies, encompassing its vast diversity from the origins of the Kievan state to Putin's Russia. Each book is intended for a broad range of readers, covers a side of Russian history and culture that has not been well-understood, and is meant to stimulate conversation.

Published Titles

Upcoming Titles

THE SOVIET GULAG

HISTORY AND MEMORY

Jeffrey S. Hardy

BLOOMSBURY ACADEMIC
LONDON • NEW YORK • OXFORD • NEW DELHI • SYDNEY

BLOOMSBURY ACADEMIC
Bloomsbury Publishing Plc
50 Bedford Square, London, WC1B 3DP, UK
1385 Broadway, New York, NY 10018, USA
29 Earlsfort Terrace, Dublin 2, Ireland

BLOOMSBURY, BLOOMSBURY ACADEMIC and the Diana logo
are trademarks of Bloomsbury Publishing Plc

First published in Great Britain 2022

Cover image: © White Sea—Baltic Sea Construction,
Universal History Archive/Contributor

A catalogue record for this book is available from the British Library.

A catalog record for this book is available from the Library of Congress.

ISBN: HB: 978-1-3501-2819-4
          PB: 978-1-3501-2818-7
          ePDF: 978-1-3501-2820-0
          eBook: 978-1-3501-2821-7

Typeset by Integra Software Services Pvt. Ltd.
Printed and bound in Great Britain

To find out more about our authors and books visit www.bloomsbury.com
and sign up for our newsletters.

CONTENTS

FIGURES

PREFACE

Over the past twenty or so years I have been asked some tough questions about my research: Why study the Gulag? How do you not get depressed when reading about all the suffering, torture, and death? To these I sometimes add a similar question, usually while sitting in a snow-blasted post-Soviet archive: why not research the historical development of tourism infrastructure in the Caribbean, or the history of fishing in the South Pacific? These questions are not easy to answer. Like other difficult historical topics such as the Holocaust, the Gulag as an object of study requires not only intellectual justification but also a very personal explanation. Tacitly implied in the questions, after all, is a psychological interrogation: what kind of person would choose to devote many years of their life to something so morbid?

Let me start with the intellectual justification. To me, the Gulag is important to study for three reasons. First, it teaches us about one of the largest and most important countries of the twentieth century. The Soviet Union was a radical and unprecedented experiment in the large-scale construction of socialism, which forced, assisted, or inspired socialist revolutions around the world. While the construction of socialism was in many ways an optimistic dream about the potential of human society, a component part of this experiment was the intense repression of enemies and potential enemies. Mass killings, forced starvation, and the highest rate of imprisonment the world had ever seen were as much a part of the USSR as victory in the Second World War or Yuri Gagarin's flight into space. The Gulag was, in other words, a cornerstone institution of an ideological and geopolitical superpower.

Second, the Gulag is important to understanding Russia and other post-Soviet states today. The sheer size of the Gulag meant that almost everyone in the USSR knew someone who had served time or died there, and that memory is still active in post-Soviet society. Museums and monuments dedicated to the Gulag dot the post-Soviet landscape. Moreover, the Russian penal system today is often compared to its predecessor, the Gulag; it too is large and violent, and it also holds political opponents who were repressed by an authoritarian state. The Gulag thus forms an integral part of the contested Soviet legacy, as state bodies, nongovernmental organizations, and private individuals debate how or even if to commemorate the victims of the Gulag.

Finally, the Gulag is important to study because it teaches us about the human condition; it forces us to confront our capacities for good and for evil. In this pressure-cooker institution of control and correction, a wide range of motives, emotions, and behaviors are evident. There are stories of sadistic torture; of ideologically inspired violence; and of starvation, rape, and murder. But there are also accounts of intense friendships, hope, kindness, and love. The Gulag was a place of music, communion with nature, poetry, and worship. It was also a place of mass graves, gang warfare, and back-breaking labor in extreme Siberian winters. No wonder the Gulag provided the subject matter for great works of memoir and literature, which inspire and caution modern audiences the world over.

As for my own personal justification for studying the Gulag, I am still figuring that out. I could point to my reading of Aleksandr Solzhenitsyn's works as a high-school student, which prompted an early fascination with a world that seemed so foreign compared to my comfortable teenage life in a middle-class suburban town. I could certainly reflect on my months as a Christian missionary in Magadan (the "capital of the Gulag"), where I visited museums and monuments dedicated to the Gulag and talked with some of the descendants of Gulag inmates. And I could, perhaps, blame one of my early advisers who, hearing of my interest in the Gulag, encouraged me to write my Master's thesis on that topic. It was something that mattered and still needed to be told in its full complexity, he said. And that is what I have been trying to do ever since. Yes, it is difficult sometimes. You never do become fully desensitized to the accounts of human depravity that litter the memoirs and archival records of the Gulag. But then you never cease to marvel at the occasional moments of light and love, of joy and beauty.

What follows is a history of the Gulag and an account of its contested memory in post-Soviet Russia. In addition to the basic facts, I discuss how historians have approached the Gulag from different angles and have, at times, come to varying conclusions. Given the enormity and complexity of the Gulag, it is no surprise that there are interpretive differences among those who study it, just as there were among those who lived it. By the end of this book, I hope that you will have a greater appreciation for what the Gulag was and why it still matters today. If you are interested in learning more about a particular topic or time period, please consult the endnotes and select bibliography. Though not exhaustive, they afford an excellent starting point for further investigation.

No book, not even short ones like this, is a product of one person's effort. I have many friends and colleagues to thank for their contributions to my understanding of the Gulag, including Steve Barnes, Alan Barenberg, Emily Johnson, Wilson Bell, Judith Pallot, Marc Elie, and Stephen Kotkin. Stephen Norris encouraged me to write this book and Rhodri Mogford and his team at Bloomsbury were supportive at every step of the process. My research assistant Michael Green was indispensable in the final stages of writing and editing. Finally, thank you to my wife Pam, for her unflagging support in all my pursuits.

INTRODUCTION

On October 30, 2017, President Vladimir Putin of Russia and Patriarch Kirill of the Russian Orthodox Church dedicated the Wall of Grief, a large monument to victims of political repression in the Union of Soviet Socialist Republics (hereafter USSR or Soviet Union). Located in downtown Moscow, the wall depicts in abstract form a bronze mass of suffering people, while two detached stelae in front display the word "remember" carved in numerous languages. This memorial was funded largely by the Russian government. Its placement on a busy downtown intersection was designed to affirm that, in the words of President Putin, the Russian people "remember the tragedy of [the] repressions and the reasons that caused them." He further explained that regardless of anything positive the Soviet Union achieved, the crimes of that era "cannot be justified in any way." Many Russians were pleased that such a project had been completed. According to the director of the nearby State Museum of Gulag History, "the fact that this is taking place by presidential decree and is supported by ordinary citizens, who gave money for the monument, indicates to me that this is a new point of reckoning." But others were less sanguine, seeing it as a way for Putin to distract from his own civil rights abuses. As one group of opponents of the regime declared, the monument only provided a pretext "to pretend that political repression is a thing long since past"[1] [Figure 1].

These conflicting views of the Wall of Grief help illustrate how contested historical memory is in Russia today. So too does the controversial decision by the Russian state just four years after the erection of the Wall of Grief to liquidate the Memorial Society, the most important non-governmental organization devoted to preserving the memory of Soviet repression. Accused of "distorting

Figure I.1 Wall of Grief, Moscow.

history" and of hiding foreign sources of funding, it was ordered to cease operations on December 28, 2021.[2] Without societies such as Memorial, which managed libraries, museums, monuments, and educational programming across Russia, the USSR's legacy of political murder, famine, mass incarceration, and forced labor will no doubt become more distant and abstract, as abstract as the formless people carved into the Wall of Grief. And perhaps this is precisely what Putin wants.

But enough, for now at least, about memory in post-Soviet Russia. We will return to this topic in Chapter 6. First, we need to understand what is being remembered, or misremembered, or forgotten altogether.

This is a book about one of the cornerstone institutions of Soviet repression, the Gulag. Before proceeding further, we need to establish what the Gulag was. It is a term that has been defined both narrowly and broadly, and that has been applied to a wide range of contexts beyond the Soviet Union. Strictly speaking, Gulag is a Stalin-era acronym for the Main Administration of Camps. This was an organization within the Soviet secret police apparatus tasked with imprisoning convicts, engaging them in "socially beneficial" labor, and reforming them into "honest Soviet citizens." In its most basic definition, the Gulag was the Soviet Union's penal system, the Soviet corollary to the prison systems of Europe and North America.

Yet the Gulag defies such a simple definition. For one thing, many Gulag prisoners were sent there not by Soviet courts but by extra-judicial organs of repression. For another thing, the primary places of imprisonment were not prisons; rather, most inmates served in camps or colonies (smaller versions of the camps) that were located all over the Soviet Union and especially in the sparsely populated regions of the Far North, the Urals, Siberia, Kazakhstan, and the Far East. And the location mattered—these were labor camps explicitly designed to contribute to economic development. Finally, there is the fact that millions of people died in the Gulag, not because they were sentenced to death, but because they starved, froze, succumbed to illness, or were victims of physical violence. Most prison systems are to some extent grounded in violence and deprivation, but the scale of mortality in the Gulag is impossible to ignore when thinking about how to define it.

To sum up, this was no simple institution. The Gulag was as much a concentration camp system as it was a penal system. It was a vast network, an "archipelago" of camps, colonies, and prisons, to which a broad range of common criminals, political dissenters, class enemies, and other suspected opponents of the Soviet regime were sent.[3] Its mission was not just to isolate or rehabilitate, it was to build railroads, mine coal, and grow crops. And perhaps, as some scholars and survivors have charged, its mission, at least during the reign of Joseph Stalin, was to kill or at minimum preside over the deaths of those unworthy to remain Soviet citizens.

To complicate matters further, the term "Gulag" has sometimes been used to encompass a wider array of institutions and practices related to punishment in the USSR. Especially in the first three decades of Soviet power, a range of extra-judicial repressive measures were used, including forced starvation, torture, and summary execution. Internal exile and capital punishment were employed for most of the Soviet Union's existence. More lenient forms of judicial sanction included monetary fines and forced labor without incarceration. And even free citizens in the Soviet Union lived a constrained existence, with restrictions on movement, speech, and other civil liberties, along with intense pressure to think and behave in ways prescribed by the Communist Party. The entire Soviet Union was, in this more expansive sense, part of the Gulag.[4]

Even more broadly, the term "Gulag" has been applied in rhetorical fashion to a range of contexts the world over, typically with the connotation that these are places of repression and excess death. Often these are penal systems in the communist world—China, North Korea, Cuba, etc.—but a quick scan of your local university's library catalog will also reveal references to colonial repression in Kenya and the prison industry in the United States. The term has even been extended metaphorically to public schools and gated communities. I will leave it up to the reader to determine if the provocative application of the term Gulag to these various contexts is insightful or only designed to grab attention.

This book is not about colonial Kenya or the United States; rather, it is about the Gulag in the narrow sense of the Soviet Union's prison-camp system. In two ways, however, its coverage will be more expansive. First, the Gulag was officially created by Stalin in 1929 and continued to exist until the collapse of the Soviet Union, although its name, structure, and to some extent purpose were periodically changed. But this book will also address the pre-Gulag penal-camp system of 1917–29 in order to show the Gulag's intellectual and institutional origins. Second, this book will explore the use of capital punishment and internal exile, in particular the Stalin-era "special settlements" that in important ways resembled the Gulag.

****

Before proceeding to Chapter 1 and the Bolshevik Revolution of 1917, I present here a bit of background on judicial punishment and incarceration before that point, both in Russia and in Europe more broadly. The Gulag and its related institutions did not emerge out of a vacuum, nor were they strictly a product of the Marxist ideology that Vladimir Lenin and his fellow Bolsheviks so ardently preached. Although ideology and the specificities of the Soviet Union were important factors in the creation of the Gulag, this seminal Soviet institution also rested on the foundation of three existing institutions: exile, the penitentiary, and the concentration camp.

Exile is the age-old practice of expelling a member of a community who had committed a crime or otherwise violated a societal norm. It has taken various forms but typically refers to forced relocation, often to a remote area, within a nation-state or empire. The UK in the eighteenth century exiled convicts to its North American colonies and then in the nineteenth century to Australia; it also exiled people from British India to the Andaman Islands in the Indian Ocean. France exiled prisoners to New Caledonia and French Guiana; Portugal exiled people to Angola; and Denmark sent them to its Caribbean holdings. The basic point of exile was to cleanse society of undesirable elements, especially convicted felons, but it was also employed to make use of available labor power or else to force exiles into programs of political re-education.[5]

The Russian Empire was among the most enthusiastic practitioners of exile. In a process that began in the 1500s and developed into a mass institution in the 1800s, Russian authorities exiled a wide array of convicts, political prisoners, Polish rebels, religious dissenters, and village ne'er-do-wells to Siberia and Sakhalin Island.[6] Many Bolsheviks and other socialists in the late 1800s and early 1900s were subjected to Siberian exile, including both Vladimir Lenin and Joseph Stalin (Lenin subsequently enjoyed a life of self-imposed exile in Western Europe). Exile in the Russian Empire was varied and often contradictory, plagued by violence, incompetence, and incongruous aims—it was at once supposed to cleanse society, punish malefactors, reform criminals, and economically develop Siberia. Some exiles were forced to perform hard labor while others were told to find work themselves. Some were held in prisons or camp-type institutions while others lived in villages among free citizens. Many escaped back to European Russia (Stalin among them), others served their full sentences and were then allowed to return (Lenin did this), and some violently revolted against what they viewed as an unjust system. But a large number of Siberian exiles, along with family members who often accompanied them, died prematurely from violence, disease, and exhaustion.

The contradictions of exile and the growing sense that it was unsuited for a modern society eventually led many in the Russian empire to call for its abolition. Some criticized its violence and inefficiency, others that it failed to accomplish the goals of isolation or of turning exiles into productive members of society.[7] Yet Siberian exile was ultimately preserved. In fact, exile was used extensively during the First World War when the Russian Empire deported over 200,000 ethnic Germans away from the theater of operations to various points in Siberia, Central Asia, and the Far North.[8] Most European states, by contrast, abandoned or sharply curtailed the practice before the outbreak of the First World War.

Part of the reason for this shift away from exile in Europe was the development of new penitentiary systems, which were supposedly more humane and rational alternatives to exile, capital punishment, and various types of corporal punishment (whipping, branding, pillory) that were common judicial sentences in the early modern era. Forcibly putting people in confined spaces as punishment has a history stretching back thousands of years and compelling such people to work has a history almost as long. However, imprisonment was not a dominant form of punishment until the 1800s, when the modern penitentiary gained prominence in Europe and North America.

In contrast to corporal and capital punishment, the central point of the penitentiary was not to exact retribution or deter people from committing crimes, but to turn criminals into obedient and productive citizens. There was much debate in Europe and the United States about how precisely to accomplish the correction and re-training of inmates, but it usually involved a mix of education, religious practice, repetitive labor tasks, strict rules governing behavior, and various punishments for failing to obey those rules. By the early 1900s, penitentiaries were becoming more specialized—each focusing on a particular type of offender—and new policies and programs such as parole (conditional early release) and vocational training centered on preparing inmates to re-enter society. Not everyone subscribed to the idea of correctional reform. Conservative policy makers and prison officials often insisted on the principle of "less eligibility," arguing that prisons should provide worse living conditions than those available to the poorest in free society in order to deter people from crime. This focus on deterrence (and retribution) clashed with the aim of correction and at times resulted in contradictory policies concerning penitentiaries and their inmates.[9] Not surprisingly, there was (and still is) skepticism regarding how well penitentiaries reformed people or deterred potential criminals.

In the Russian Empire, the dominance of the exile system and corporal punishment (flogging as a judicial punishment was forbidden only in 1904), coupled with the high cost of constructing and staffing penitentiaries, meant that few were built before 1917. It was only in 1895 that the Ministry of Internal Affairs acknowledged that prisons oriented around correction were the "primary weapon in the struggle against crime" and expressed the hope that convicts after release would be prepared to return "to honorable and respectable lives."[10] Employing a program of labor, education, religious devotion, and visits by well-meaning private citizens, Russian penitentiaries were explicitly modeled on their Western European counterparts. As in the West, though, there was persistent debate about how harsh prison conditions should be, with one conservative official arguing that prison conditions should be sufficiently harsh as to "destroy the desire of criminals to commit a second crime."[11] In any case, while most convicted felons in the Russian Empire continued to be sent to Siberia rather than a Western-style penitentiary, these penitentiaries existed and were inherited by the Bolshevik regime in 1917.

The final institution that laid the groundwork for the Gulag was the concentration camp. In contrast to the penitentiary and exile, this was a recent invention, only a few decades old when the Bolsheviks took power. The purpose of a concentration camp was to detain citizens who had not been accused, let alone convicted, of a specific crime, but who were suspected of being in a position to provide aid to an enemy military or paramilitary force. Concentration camps were developed in the colonial setting of the late 1800s and early 1900s, employed by Spain against Cubans, the British Empire against the Boers and their allies in South Africa (with separate concentration camps for whites and Blacks), and the United States against Filipinos. In all cases it was a temporary tool designed to repress populations that were actively opposing colonial rule or were at least suspected of such.[12]

Concentration camps were then used by all belligerents during the First World War as the concept of "total war" meant that civilians as well as soldiers were targeted for incapacitation to stop them from contributing to the war effort. Close to 1 million civilians were incarcerated, primarily men who were thus prevented from joining the war effort, but also women and children. Russia made little use of concentration camps for civilians, despite calls from some high-ranking officers to detain enemy subjects in concentration camps.[13] Most of the thousands of enemy subjects detained by Russian forces, rather, were subjected to conditions of exile that involved monitoring but not confinement in an actual camp. But like all belligerents, Russia did make extensive use of prisoner-of-war camps, which held tens of thousands of enemy combatants at the collapse of the Romanov Dynasty in 1917.

I share this background to show that when the Bolsheviks took power in 1917, they inherited specific institutions and ideas about punishment and state power from the immediate context of the Russian Empire. But they also had at their fingertips the broader European framework of exile, penitentiaries, and concentration camps. Lenin and other top Bolsheviks, after all, spent years in self-imposed exile in Switzerland, France, England, Italy, and Germany, and were familiar with their political and police structures. They understood that the world in 1917 was one in which states actively managed their populations through programs of reform, forced labor, exclusion, and incapacitation. As we shall see in the following chapters, these ideas and institutions, tools in a non-ideological governing toolbox, were readily incorporated into the governing matrix of Marxist ideology and Soviet statecraft.

CHAPTER 1
REVOLUTIONARY DREAMS AND
EARLY SOVIET CONFINEMENT

The preeminent chronicler of the Gulag was Aleksandr Solzhenitsyn. Imprisoned from 1945 to 1953 and then exiled to Kazakhstan until 1956, he devoted much of the rest of his life to collecting first-hand accounts of the Gulag and writing about the exploitative system that he and so many others endured. He was eventually expelled from the Soviet Union, but even before this he began publishing his monumental three-volume *Gulag Archipelago* in the West. Though mostly about the crimes of the Stalin era, Solzhenitsyn also endeavored to uncover the early history of, as he metaphorically termed it, "our sewage disposal system."[1] Where did the Gulag come from? What was its original purpose? And how did it acquire its distinctive features?

This chapter will attempt to answer those questions, looking at Soviet incarceration from the Bolshevik Revolution of 1917 to the actual creation of the Gulag in 1929. Solzhenitsyn viewed this era as one of "consistent, cold-blooded planning and never-weakening persistence" in pursuit of the brutally repressive system of confinement that flowered in the 1930s.[2] But thanks to additional research conducted after the opening of Soviet archives in the 1990s, we now know that the pre-history of the Gulag was not quite so simple, the proverbial line from Bolshevism to Stalinism not quite so straight. In fact, the 1920s were as much a period of confusion, contradiction, and reaction when it came to penal policy and practice as they were of cunning calculation.

Revolution, Civil War, and the Makings of Soviet Penal Policy

The last Romanov emperor, Nicholas II, abdicated in March 1917 amidst societal collapse produced by Russia's losing efforts in the First World War and Nicholas's own inept leadership. The so-called Provisional Government that replaced him continued fighting the war, faring just as poorly against the German army. It also failed to reestablish social order, with crime increasing dramatically in the spring and summer of 1917. Even the capital city of Petrograd (now Saint Petersburg) was wracked with theft, assault, gang warfare, and murder.[3] It was in this moment of chaos and criminality that Vladimir Lenin and his fellow Bolsheviks successfully carried out a coup d'état in November 1917 that brought down the provisional government and ushered in a radical Marxist regime.

Lenin quickly found that imposing socialism on a war-torn country on the verge of complete socio-economic collapse was far more difficult than criticizing the Tsar from the cafes of Switzerland. Even leaving aside the catastrophic state of the country, Marxist socialism had never been attempted on a mass scale; it had always been a theoretical, and therefore ambiguous, program, and not everyone agreed on what it was or how to bring it about. From the beginning and well into the 1920s, policies and programs were often contradictory or fleeting, issued one week and rescinded the next. Central and local officials clashed on how to interpret and implement decrees. Improvisation often trumped calculation when it came to much of Soviet governance during this early period.

Further complicating this quest to build socialism was a stark reality: everywhere the Bolsheviks looked they saw enemies. One set of enemies—German soldiers—they managed to eliminate by concluding a separate peace with Germany in March 1918. Another set of enemies—the ordinary criminals that had helped create such an incendiary situation in 1917—continued to thieve, rob, and murder without regard for the socialist ideals proclaimed by Lenin's new regime. Marxist theorists had long viewed ordinary crime as the product of class-based economic exploitation and improper education. As socialism was built, a "withering away of crime" was supposed to occur and communism, a sort of far-off utopian dream, would then feature a virtually crime-free society. This must have been hard to imagine as Bolshevik officials, including Lenin himself, were targeted by both criminal syndicates and ordinary muggers looking to get rich off their new political masters.

Other enemies to Soviet power came in the form of nationalists who wanted political independence for Poland, Finland, Ukraine, Georgia, and various other parts of the former Russian Empire. Church officials representing Orthodoxy, Islam, and every other denomination made no secret of their hatred for the Bolsheviks and their anti-religious attitudes. There were class-based enemies— the nobility and bourgeoisie (the middle class)—who in Marxist ideology represented the old economic orders of feudalism and capitalism and whose very existence prevented the creation of a classless socialist society. Finally, the Bolsheviks faced an array of ideological opponents, including monarchists, liberals, and various non-Bolshevik socialists. Some demanded participation in Lenin's new government, while others plotted to overthrow it. Even before the Soviet regime celebrated its first birthday, it was flung into a bloody civil war that the Bolshevik "red" army only managed to win against the various "white" forces in 1921.

So other than wage war against "white" armies, what could the Bolsheviks do with this dizzying array of enemies that threatened their political survival and prevented the creation of a socialist society? One answer was simply to eliminate them from society by killing them. Capital punishment had featured prominently in the tsarist judicial system, particularly in the aftermath of the 1905 revolution when it was employed against thousands of socialists. After the fall of the Romanov Dynasty in early 1917, the death penalty was abolished by the Provisional Government but reinstated a short time later. The Bolsheviks followed a similar pattern, abolishing it in November 1917 before reintroducing it after just four months (while employing summary execution against certain criminals even when it was forbidden by law). Thus, when faced with the challenge of governing, both the liberal Provisional Government and Lenin's Bolsheviks found capital punishment a useful tool to cleanse society by violence and thereby deter others from crime.

Over the following years of civil war, the Soviet secret police, known initially as the *Cheka* (short for the All-Russian Extraordinary Commission for Combating Counterrevolution and Sabotage), was vigorous in handing down death sentences that could not be appealed, but the regular court system also mandated capital punishment in many cases. The *Cheka* and Red Army also perpetrated summary executions without trial. In all, somewhere between 60,000 and 100,000 people were executed in the first three years of Soviet power.[4] In 1920, the death penalty was suspended, except for rare cases prosecuted by military tribunals, but then reinstated as "an exceptional measure" for the gravest political crimes in the 1922 Criminal Code. Many Bolsheviks were clearly uncomfortable with the death penalty on a theoretical level but felt compelled to use it as a matter of practicality.

Most people targeted as enemies of the Soviet regime, however, were not killed. Soviet courts handed out a large number of minor punishments—fines, suspended sentences, confiscation of property, compulsory labor, and so forth—for lesser crimes. Indeed, there was a commitment among many leading Bolsheviks to be lenient in relation to crimes committed by workers and peasants, and this was consistent with "progressive" penal theory popular in European reformist circles that aimed at reducing the use of imprisonment. Soviet courts also made limited use of exile, banishing church authorities and political opponents to remote locations within Soviet Russia. This was significant as the Provisional Government of 1917 had just recently abolished the centuries-old system of Siberian exile.

Between capital punishment and various milder sanctions stood incarceration. When the Tsarist regime collapsed there were close to 150,000 inmates in the prison system, although around a third of these were awaiting trial.[5] The Provisional Government of 1917 freed the vast majority of these inmates in a mass amnesty and was sparing in making new arrests, owing in part to a lack of state capacity in the chaotic situation of 1917. This meant the Bolsheviks inherited numerous prisons but only around 35,000 inmates in late 1917.[6] They also inherited the prisoner-of-war camps and concentration camps associated with the First World War. During the initial years of Soviet power, many people were sent to these prisons and camps, and increasingly to newly established camps: "special designation" camps, "concentration" camps, and "forced labor" camps. Camps, as opposed to prisons, had the advantage of being quick and inexpensive to set up. Some were simple affairs hastily thrown together with barbed wire and tents. Others were located in monasteries and convents seized in the Bolsheviks' initial war against religion. These had been used over the previous centuries to imprison certain categories of offenders, and the new regime found them suitable for this purpose as well. After all, they had walls, cells, and a whole array of buildings (dining halls, kitchens, workshops, etc.) designed for self-sufficient operation.

Data on the number of penal facilities and inmates for the early years of Soviet power is scattered and sometimes difficult to decipher, but there can be no doubt that a dramatic expansion of the penal system occurred by the end of 1920, with hundreds of prisons and camps holding at least 150,000 inmates. By early 1922 that figure exceeded 200,000.[7] Interestingly, these institutions and their inmates were managed by three different government agencies. The People's Commissariat of Justice operated prisons holding those sentenced by regular courts; the People's Commissariat of Internal Affairs (NKVD) operated "forced labor" camps for those sentenced by regular courts; and the *Cheka* operated both prisons and camps for those that it imprisoned itself. These lines, however, were often blurred, especially as the *Cheka* sentenced more people than its facilities could hold. It was an institutional mess, in other words, marked by bureaucratic infighting among the three agencies tasked with incarcerating criminals and enemies of Soviet power.

As for the prisons and camps themselves, a distinguishing feature during the years of civil war was improvisation and chaos. Penal facilities were typically overcrowded and suffered from a lack of food and supplies. Prisoners often went in and out of prisons seemingly at will. Turnover and corruption among staff were high. Orders from various administrative bodies were frequent and contradictory, and resources needed to implement such orders were rarely provided. Prison and camp directors and other personnel often acted independently, without regard to instructions from Moscow. And even those in charge had little idea as to how to convert the penal system into something consistent with Marxist ideology. Lenin and his fellow revolutionaries in foreign exile, it turned out, had not thought much about operating a socialist penal system.

To take just one example to illustrate the variable nature of early Soviet prisons, some prison bosses immediately shut down all religious worship services for inmates in the name of creating a socialist society free from antiquated superstitions. But others continued to allow them, citing the new regime's insistence on the freedom of religion and the desire of many inmates and guards to worship. Central prison authorities in Moscow, when pressed on this matter in 1919, allowed this variability of practices to continue well into the 1920s. Little wonder that some prisoners during this chaotic period wrote of a lenient and humane penal regime while others complained of starvation, torture, and humiliation. Both were true.

Despite this general impression of chaos and improvisation, three central themes emerged in the operation of Soviet Russia's prisons and camps: re-education, economic self-sufficiency, and retribution. Not surprisingly, these were three of the central features of European penitentiary, exile, and concentration camp systems. The Bolsheviks, after all, inherited not just institutions but ideas and practices from the tsarist regime, which in turn had relied on pan-European models of imprisonment. These were ideas that transcended ideological and political lines, that could be used by socialists, fascists, and democratic capitalists alike.

Re-education was the central idea behind penitentiary construction in Europe in the 1800s and was quickly adopted by the Soviet regime. Early on, it was promoted most heavily by the People's Commissariat of Justice, which viewed re-education as one of its primary aims and which attempted to organize educational classes and propaganda for its inmates. But scarce resources meant that little if anything toward this end was accomplished in the first years of Soviet power. In fact, there is strong evidence to suggest that Lenin and other top Bolsheviks were uninterested in pursuing a comprehensive program of re-education in prison while they were struggling to win the civil war. One central aspect of re-education that was employed, however, was labor. Hard labor, repetitive labor, or vocational training had long been used in various prisons and camps in Europe, often with the goal of turning supposedly lazy or untrained criminals into productive workers upon release. Already in January 1918 the People's Commissariat of Justice ordered that inmates be forced to perform labor, a decree consistent with Lenin's oft-quoted Biblical and socialist mantra of "if anyone will not work, neither shall he eat."[8] The *Cheka* and NKVD likewise forced inmates to work in their prisons and camps.

But while labor was certainly seen by some as a key re-educational device, as evidenced by the early adoption of the term "corrective labor," more often in this time period it was a way to make imprisonment financially self-sufficient. This second aim of prison systems, making inmates pay for their own imprisonment so as to not burden state budgets, was a common goal of European exile and penitentiary systems. For the early Soviet era this impulse was particularly pronounced in the *Cheka* and NKVD, but was also a concern for the Commissariat of Justice. With money and resources tight across all Soviet agencies, prisons and camps were ordered to finance their operations out of the production of their inmates. "Freeing themselves from state support" was a prime argument made by NKVD authorities in their power struggle against the Commissariat of Justice.[9] The chaotic nature of the early regime meant that penal officials often could not find work for their inmates to perform, but it is notable that forced labor in pursuit of fiscal aims was a feature of Soviet imprisonment from the beginning [Figure 1.1].

The final primary goal of early Soviet penal facilities, particularly those run by the *Cheka* and the NKVD, was retribution. If the Commissariat of Justice was staffed by traditional legal experts who looked to continue the best practices of European jurisprudence, the *Cheka* and NKVD were led by revolutionaries who viewed terror as an important tool in the civil war.[10] Inmates in the *Cheka* camps of the Far North in particular were starved, beaten, and summarily shot, all at the whim of camp administrators and guards. Those who managed to survive, as one memoirist related, were turned "into pitiful, intimidated slaves."[11] Other factors fed into these conditions.

Figure 1.1 Inmates at work at the Taganka Prison, Moscow, 1920s.

Food and other resources were scarce; camp employment attracted those already inclined to violence; and some camp guards and administrators displayed a revolutionary zeal for carrying out a brutal, ideologically inspired program of class warfare. This was an important departure even from the principle of "less eligibility" promoted in some European prisons in the nineteenth century, which mandated that conditions in prisons must be worse than those endured by the working poor. While violence is often endemic in penal systems, retribution meted out against prisoners was, for some Bolshevik officials, a feature rather than a defect in the system.

Stabilization in the 1920s

After the civil war ended with Bolshevik victory in 1921, the Soviet party-state stabilized as Lenin pursued policies oriented toward centralizing political power, rebuilding the economy, and developing a socialist society. A new constitution was adopted in January 1924 that formally created the Union of Soviet Socialist Republics (USSR) out of the ashes of the old Russian Empire. That same month, Vladimir Lenin, who had suffered ill health for years, died and was entombed on Red Square (where he remains to this day). Joseph Stalin, Leon Trotsky, and others engaged in a fierce succession struggle over the following years, which Stalin eventually won. While his power was relatively insecure, however, he did little to substantially alter the system that his patron, Lenin, had erected.

In the penal sphere, stabilization after the civil war meant bureaucratic consolidation, with the NKVD winning its power struggle against the People's Commissariat of Justice and taking over operation of its prisons. In terms of ideas, this move seems to have signaled a preference by Soviet leaders for hard labor, financial self-sufficiency, and retribution rather than leniency and re-education, but this was not actually the case. For one thing, the Criminal Code of 1922 ensured that most sentences to incarceration were short, usually under a year. Leniency, rather than retribution, was the guiding principle of this code, which remained in force throughout the decade. One imprisoned member of an opposition political party, for instance, recalled a very lax regime at Moscow's famous Butyrka prison, where inmates freely mingled, received visitors, ate food from care packages, exercised, played chess, read socialist literature, and openly debated the nature of the Bolshevik Revolution. The prison authorities, meanwhile, treated the inmates with respect during this "brief, idyllic period," as she remembered it.[12]

But it was not just leniency that was promoted by the NKVD in the 1920s. The new director of the NKVD's Main Administration of Places of Confinement, Yevsey Shirvindt, soon renamed prisons "houses of correction" and took concrete steps to emphasize re-education rather than retribution. Newspapers and literary journals produced by inmates flourished, prison libraries were stocked with books, educational classes were organized, and workshops devoted to vocational training were assembled. Even the official vocabulary changed to reflect this new focus on re-education rather than retribution.[13] With the intense pressures of the civil war seemingly behind them, many penal officials in the 1920s took seriously the charge to prepare their inmates for an honest and productive life after release.

The philosophical debate over the aims of imprisonment continued to be fought over the following years. A set of instructions issued in

1924 titled "Guiding Principles of Criminal Legislation" reflected the desire for both re-education and self-sufficiency. Notably absent was any mention of retribution or class warfare. Still, those ideas did not disappear completely. As Vladimir Tolmachev, who became head of the NKVD in 1928, argued, "Imprisonment should be a frightening experience .... Our class enemies should be put in especially difficult conditions."[14] With Stalin's power secure and new plans for social transformation well in the works, the pendulum among some penal officials was shifting back to retribution. A central conclusion here is that the Soviet penal establishment in the 1920s had difficulty figuring out which of the aims of imprisonment to emphasize. It was an ongoing negotiation and certainly did not follow a preconceived plan.

Stabilization in the 1920s after years of civil war also meant a relatively constant inmate population. Crime persisted, as did political opposition to the Soviet regime, and the Soviets continued to embrace class warfare—judges were instructed in the 1924 criminal code, for instance, to give harsher punishment to the "exploiting classes." However, there were no major waves of repression until the end of the decade, and capital punishment was used sparingly. Moreover, lenient sentencing guidelines meant that in the mid-1920s just 20 percent of convicts were sentenced to terms of imprisonment, with the rest receiving milder sanctions.[15] This resulted in a stable number of inmates that in 1926 numbered around 200,000 (not counting tens of thousands held by the secret police, which will be discussed below). The average sentence, meanwhile, was only 0.72 years and liberal use of parole and amnesty meant that inmates typically served less than three-fourths of their term.[16] Despite this, penal facilities were often overcrowded, with the cash-strapped Soviet state unwilling to build new houses of correction. After all, funding for necessary programs like education was in short supply, and if crime was eventually supposed to wither away, there was no ideological impetus to build new prisons.

This lack of funding and the ongoing confusion concerning the central mission of prisons and camps meant that many problems persisted. One in particular was the inability of most prison bosses to provide sufficient work for their inmates, which the NKVD harshly criticized in a 1925 circular as "depriving the inmates of the benefits of corrective labor, i.e. the places of incarceration are failing to accomplish their primary mission as defined in the Corrective Labor Code."[17] Another problem was difficulty in instituting a progressive system of imprisonment that moved well-behaved inmates to gradually less restrictive conditions of imprisonment in order to prepare them for reintegration into society. Popular in the West, this was pursued by the People's Commissariat of Justice already during the civil war and continued to be official policy under NKVD management in the 1920s. But overcrowding and a lack of funding meant that most penal institutions only partially implemented this program.

As late as 1928 the Soviet government pursued a lenient penal policy for those sentenced by regular Soviet courts. Police were instructed to ignore certain categories of small-scale crime, judges were told to avoid incarceration (and certainly execution) in favor of lesser punishments, and penal officials were asked to make more liberal use of parole and "temporary absences" (where inmates were allowed to return home for a short period of time before returning to the house of correction). Shortly after this, however, the political climate in the country turned decisively toward policies of class conflict, retribution, and breakneck economic development. As we will see in the next chapter, this would have widespread ramifications on the penal system, particularly as the Soviet state turned to the secret police to run the Soviet penal system, a choice rooted in what was happening at Solovki in the 1920s.

Solovki

The most important development related to the Gulag in the 1920s was the creation of the Solovetsky Camp of Forced Labor of Special Significance (SLON). This camp was located on the Solovetsky Islands, a small archipelago in the White Sea that had boasted a prominent monastery since the 1400s. Considered one of the holiest sites of Russian Orthodoxy, the monastery was seized and desecrated by the Bolsheviks in 1920 and the islands were identified as an ideal location for holding prisoners. "The harsh environment, the work regime, the fight against the forces of nature will be a good school for all criminal elements," the Bolshevik newspaper *Izvestia* declared.[18] Just a few years later, on October 13, 1923, SLON was created by the Soviet secret police (which was renamed the Joint State Political Directorate, or OGPU, that same year). While the monastery had held some prisoners in the centuries before 1917, the OGPU in the 1920s converted the islands into a massive penal camp populated by tens of thousands of inmates. It was the largest penal institution of the decade and paved the way, in its size, purpose, and deep contradictions, for the Gulag.

SLON was the primary destination for both criminal and political prisoners convicted and sentenced by the OGPU (rather than the regular court system). Inmates were housed in a variety of locations: hastily constructed barracks, cells formerly occupied by monks, and even the Cathedral of the Transfiguration and other chapels. For the first few years, socialist and anarchist political prisoners who had fought against the tsarist regime but then opposed Bolshevik rule enjoyed special status, with favorable living conditions, no mandatory labor, and packages delivered by the Political Red Cross (a sanctioned non-governmental organization devoted to aiding political prisoners in the country).[19] Like many European countries, the Soviets in these early years endeavored to keep political prisoners separate and content, and made few concerted efforts to change their ideological outlook. The situation soon deteriorated, however, and in 1925 the political prisoners were scattered among different camps and prisons and treated largely the same as the so-called counterrevolutionary prisoners: former White army officers, priests, noblemen, and prominent representatives of the capitalist bourgeoisie. This process would continue into the 1930s, when political and counterrevolutionary prisoners were targeted for the harshest repression [Figure 1.2].

With the early and temporary exception of political prisoners, the stated purpose of SLON was not substantively different from that of the Soviet Union's other penal establishments: the isolation of inmates, financial self-sufficiency, and re-education through labor and other means. These aims were not secret, nor was the existence of a massive labor camp in the White Sea; in fact, the Soviets made a

Figure 1.2 Solovki guard and inmates, 1920s.

propaganda film called *Solovki* (using guards dressed up as prisoners, some memoirists recalled) and sent famed novelist and Soviet sympathizer Maxim Gorky to the islands to write a favorable report on how the prisoners were being transformed. As Gorky concluded, in a foreshadowing of the soon-to-be-born Gulag, "It seems to me that the conclusion is clear: such camps as Solovki are necessary ... Specifically, by this method the state will reach one of its purposes: the destruction of prisons."[20] Replacing supposedly bourgeois prisons with socialist labor camps while gradually reducing the need for the labor camps through the reduction of criminality was thus the stated intention of OGPU.

The central organizing principle of life at Solovki, and the means by which financial self-sufficiency and re-education were supposed to occur, was labor. As the distinguished scholar and SLON inmate Dmitry Likhachev recalled, a picture of Lenin hung over an altar where an icon of Christ once resided, along with the inscribed slogan,

"We are showing mankind a new road. Labor will be the master of the world."[21] Inmates were organized into brigades, which worked, ate, socialized, and slept together. These brigades were assigned to a wide array of labor tasks, including logging, peat harvesting, agricultural work, and road construction. If there was still considerable debate in the West about the nature of prison labor—whether it was better to be skilled or unskilled, compulsory or voluntary—the OGPU came down decidedly on the side of forced, unskilled labor. SLON administrators often compelled their inmates to work exceedingly long hours—twelve to fourteen hours per day was not uncommon—in pursuit of self-sufficiency.

The quest for financial sustainability also meant that living conditions for inmates were difficult, with insufficient food, clothing, and medical supplies along with the harsh northern climate producing high rates of illness and mortality. Violence perpetrated by guards was also commonplace. As one group of inmates complained to Soviet authorities upon returning from Solovki to Moscow in 1926, "We went there full of energy and good health, and now we are returning as invalids, broken and crippled emotionally and physically." They then chronicled myriad abuses meted out against the inmates, including starvation rations, unbearably long working days, and summary executions.[22]

Conditions became particularly brutal starting in 1928 when former prisoner Naftaly Frenkel was given charge of SLON's economic activities. He segregated inmates based on labor productivity, raised production norms, and perfected a system of giving inmates food in correspondence to their labor output. Those who consistently failed to produce enough did not receive enough food to survive. He eliminated many of the specifically re-educational aspects of the camp in his pursuit of economic efficiency. He also began exporting much of the lumber produced by SLON prisoners to Western Europe in exchange for hard currency (which provoked outrage in the West when it was discovered). Long hours of unskilled labor in the service of the national economy would be a defining feature of the Gulag under Stalin, and it was at Solovki that this was first tested on a large scale.

But life at Solovki, particularly during the mid-1920s before Frenkel's rise, was not just about labor, privation, violence, and death. In fact, there was a surprising amount of cultural activity sanctioned by the OGPU in the name of re-education. Inmates helped produce a newspaper and monthly literary journal that were read not only by inmates but also by people all over the Soviet Union. They contained fiction, poetry, reports on current events, political cartoons, accounts of the White Sea ecosystem, updates on labor tasks, celebrations of holidays, attacks on religion, and a wide variety of other articles. A zoo and natural history museum operated with inmate curators, while other inmate specialists participated in dedicated research labs. A brass band and an orchestra staffed by prisoners regularly performed, along with choirs and other musical groups. Imprisoned directors formed theater troupes that performed both classics and new plays—comedies and melodramas among them—for inmates and guards alike. As one prisoner eloquently recalled, "The bell goes, the music dies down, the lights go out; the curtain swings open, and another world unfolds before your eyes. At this moment, if you focus attention on the stage ... you may completely forget about Solovki, forget altogether that you're a convict."[23] These cultural endeavors benefitted from the fact that many of the most talented people in the country were being locked up by the OGPU as potential enemies of the regime [Figure 1.3].

Another set of inmates brought with them a different form of culture that was tolerated to some extent, though certainly not promoted. Hundreds of Orthodox bishops, priests, monks, and nuns, along with church officials from several other religious denominations, were imprisoned at Solovki. They were often housed together and were permitted, due to their honesty, to work in trusted positions as accountants, postal employees, and warehouse guards. There was a fair amount of anti-religious propaganda conducted among inmates, including the operation of a museum of atheism. But many imprisoned Orthodox and Catholic clerics were permitted to perform and attend worship services in buildings set aside for this purpose by camp administrators. Even when not allowed to meet, it proved relatively

Figure 1.3 Solovki concert band, 1920s.

easy to worship together and to draw strength from this fellowship and their shared devotion to God. As one Orthodox inmate recalled of an inspirational Easter service, "I didn't know whether to cry or laugh from joy."[24]

That imprisoned clerics, musicians, theater directors, and writers enjoyed some level of intellectual, cultural, and even religious freedom at Solovki seems remarkable. It speaks, on one level, to the inherent contradictions in the Soviet project. A host of human rights, such as freedom of speech and conscience, were guaranteed by Soviet legislation but also routinely trampled on in the name of building socialism. Even in the secret police's penal experiment of the 1920s, such issues were not predetermined. SLON administrators could have easily forbidden religious worship and forced intellectuals to chop down trees rather than write plays and perform music. Indeed, this often did happen, particularly for those not near SLON headquarters on the main island of the Solovetsky archipelago. But many others were given a surprising amount of time and space for cultural, intellectual, and religious expression.

Of course, the intellectual, cultural, and religious expressions of these inmates were far from free. Church meetings were monitored for anti-Soviet speech and labor concerns took precedence over church attendance; plays and newspaper articles had to be kept within ideological boundaries set by SLON officials; and those participating in research centers, including the famed "Criminology Department" that studied crime and punishment, had to approach their subject matter from a Marxist perspective. The regime was eager, it seems, to instrumentalize the talents of their country's repressed intellectuals, but some of these intellectuals at Solovki managed to use their experience and knowledge in the pursuit of truth and beauty. As Dmitry Likhachev noted of his time on the archipelago, "For me the discussions with A. A. Meier and with the Solovki *intelligentsia* that revolved around him … were a second university (but first for importance)."[25] In other words, where the interests of intellectuals and cultural figures overlapped with those of SLON administrators, the product was enlightening intellectual discussion, extraordinary cultural productions, and deeply moving religious services. This would ultimately be one of the most apparent contradictions of the Gulag system: theater, music, literature, and faith coexisting alongside deprivation, violence, and death.

Perhaps not surprisingly, given the communal environment of the camp, social life for criminals continued at Solovki as well. Newspaper articles and memoirs alike describe the sub-categories and varied activities of the *shpana* (a prerevolutionary collective term for criminal prisoners), characterized by one inmate author as the "waste of the proletarian environment."[26] These inmates, who were supposed to be reformed through labor, were more often robbing other inmates, gambling, procuring alcohol by bribing the guards, and coercing other inmates into sexual relations. They spoke their own jargon and bore criminal tattoos. And while some actively cooperated with the authorities for their own gain, others formed tight-knit gangs and refused to perform any labor or otherwise cooperate with the authorities. These latter were also known for viciously policing their own society and killing "traitors" who attempted to leave their gang.[27] As we will see, this pervasive criminal activity in the camps would become one of the central aspects of social life in the Stalin-era Gulag.

Conclusions

The first years after the Bolshevik Revolution were chaotic and improvisational. Soviet authorities operated a hodge-podge system of camps and prisons, some inherited from the Old Regime and others created from scratch or out of monasteries or other existing buildings. There was little central direction from Lenin or other top Bolshevik leaders, other than the mandate to make inmates work and to figure out how to run the facilities without subsidy (neither of which was accomplished in systemic fashion). Other questions concerning organizational structure, re-education, inmate management, and so forth were left largely to the decisions of local prison bosses. Bolshevik ideology, it turned out, was quite flexible on a whole range of questions concerning crime and punishment.

The 1921–29 period witnessed some consolidation of the Soviet Union's penal systems under the People's Commissariat of Internal Affairs (NKVD) and secret police (the *Cheka*, then OGPU). The former tended to pursue many of the central tenets of Western penology, such as short sentences, the progressive system, leniency, and vocational training in the name of re-education. These were designed to be applied in particular to those deemed most reformable: the workers and peasants of the Soviet Union. The secret police's system, as exemplified by the labor camp on the Solovetsky Islands, featured longer sentences, harder labor, harsher living conditions, increased violence, and the use of large camps rather than penitentiaries. These policies were meted out primarily against political prisoners, class enemies, and the worst common criminals.

But the philosophical line between the two systems was quite blurry, as both the secret police and the NKVD were trying to figure out what punishment should look like in a socialist society. There was certainly no predetermined plan developed by Lenin or Stalin and implemented over the course of the 1920s. In fact, there was never a consensus reached on important questions such as if every prisoner was reformable and whether penal policy should emphasize leniency or harshness in pursuit of re-education or deterrence. One can certainly find in 1917–29 the origins of the Gulag system that will be discussed in the following chapters. But there is also considerable evidence for a different possibility, a more humane and less repressive path ultimately not taken.

CHAPTER 2
BUILDING THE GULAG

With his political power secure and the Soviet Union's economy recovered, Joseph Stalin announced two major transformations that would make 1929 the "year of great change." First, the USSR would pursue the forced collectivization of agriculture, and second, it would rapidly industrialize by means of a centrally planned economy. These reforms brought an end to private economic property and to the limited capitalism that had defined the 1920s. From here on, the Soviet state would exert almost total control over the economy, which it would manage through government agencies and a succession of five-year plans. For Stalin, this was both the path to socialism and to great power status in the international arena. State-led socialism would prepare the Soviet Union for potential wars with its capitalist-imperialist rivals while demonstrating to the world the superiority of the socialist system. And this would in turn prompt other nations to pursue their own socialist revolutions.

As a result of these policies and Stalin's brutal methods to achieve them, the 1930s were a chaotic decade marked by mass enthusiasm and mass suffering. Some were genuinely excited about the country's new change of direction and benefitted from increased educational opportunities and upward social mobility. While much of the world was mired in the Great Depression, the Soviet economy was booming. But the cost was steep. Living standards for many fell as economic plans prioritized heavy industry over consumer goods and housing. Construction zones and other workplaces were haphazardly organized and prone to deadly accidents. Peasants who resisted collectivization were harshly repressed. Uncompromising Soviet policies of grain extraction (exported grain helped pay for industrial technology) produced a famine that killed several million people in Ukraine, southern Russia, and Kazakhstan. Criminal codes were made harsher, which resulted in millions of people being arrested and sent to labor in the Gulag. And Stalin's deep fear of internal forces collaborating with his sworn enemy Leon Trotsky or with fascist Germany or imperialist Japan finally resulted in the Great Terror of 1937–38, in which at least 700,000 people were executed and about as many were given long terms of imprisonment.

The Gulag

So what was this Gulag to which millions of people were sent in the 1930s? In 1928 and 1929, as the number of arrests was beginning to increase, representatives of the People's Commissariat of Justice, People's Commissariat of Internal Affairs, and the secret police (OGPU) met periodically to discuss a new penal system. It quickly became clear that it would be based explicitly on the camp model, and not because it was better at re-educating inmates. As Genrikh Yagoda of the OGPU declared,

> Nobody will give money for new prisons. The construction of large camps, on the other hand—camps which will make rational use of labor—is a different matter. We have many difficulties attracting workers to the North. If we send many thousands of prisoners there, we can exploit the resources of the North .... The experience of Solovetsky shows what can be done in this area.[1]

Lumber, coal, gold, and other natural resources from sparsely settled regions were badly needed for Stalin's rapid industrialization project, and a proposed new system of labor camps was the evident solution. As Yagoda made clear, this was a system born out of the experience of Solovki that was framed in explicitly economic terms such as profitability, rationality, and labor power. Soviet citizens generally in the 1930s were treated as a labor force to mobilize and exploit, and Soviet prisoners were no exception.

The order to create this new network of labor camps was signed on June 27, 1929. It sanctioned the OGPU to build camps in the remote regions of the USSR and to "develop mineral deposits using convict labor."[2] The name of the institution created to govern the new penal system fluctuated a few times before settling on the Main Administration of Camps, typically called by its acronym, Gulag. (The precise name was periodically altered after this, but the original acronym stuck). Already by August 1930 the Gulag administered seven camps holding around 170,000 inmates. These were mostly devoted to lumber and road construction, and the OGPU was scouring the country for coal, gold, and other mineral deposits that could be exploited using forced labor. Not coincidentally, these geological expeditions were staffed heavily by prisoners, including experts in geology, mining, engineering, surveying, and other essential fields. But even if the camp model was not chosen for re-education, this does not mean that it was completely forgotten. The camps were, in fact, supposed to re-educate inmates and in 1930 the Soviet government decreed that they would be called "corrective-labor camps," a moniker that would prove more durable than previous names: concentration camp, forced labor camp, and camp of special significance.

As the Gulag expanded in the early 1930s it was given a succession of economically important projects earmarked by Stalin himself. Among the first was the White Sea—Baltic Sea Canal, with construction beginning in 1931 and lasting until 1933. This was a complex project involving a series of channels, dams, and locks that was designed to showcase the country's economic and military ambitions. Hundreds of thousands of inmates were dispatched, including many from Solovki, and like Solovki before it, the canal project was ultimately defined by stark contradictions. Living conditions for inmates were spartan, rations were often insufficient, and labor in the absence of mechanized tools was long and difficult [Figure 2.1]. Tens of thousands of inmates died due to exhaustion, disease, and violence. But there were also newspapers, brass bands, drama troupes, and political lectures in an attempt to "reforge" prisoners.[3] Inmates were meant to understand the international significance of their daily labor—they were not just building a canal, they were building socialism!—and this was supposed

Figure 2.1 Gulag prisoners building the White Sea—Baltic Sea Canal, 1933.

to motivate them to work diligently. They were also promised early release if they consistently overfulfilled their labor norms, and over ten thousand prisoners were thus freed after the canal was complete. The end result also proved to be a contradiction: after so much labor and death, the canal itself was too small and shallow to have much economic impact, nor could it be used by the Soviet navy.

Progress on the canal construction and the supposedly re-educational effect of communal labor for the greater good was trumpeted throughout the Soviet Union and abroad in newspaper articles, film clips, a play, and most notably a book co-edited by literary giant Maxim Gorky. As he declared, "The building of this canal is one of the most brilliant victories of human energy over the bitterness and wildness of nature. But it is more than that: it is also a splendidly successful attempt at the transformation of thousands of former enemies of Soviet society."[4] This was the Gulag's lofty promise that one could find in both internal and external propaganda, a mixture of socially beneficial labor, re-education, and triumph over the natural world.[5] Yet these propaganda efforts of the early 1930s would ultimately prove fleeting. Public information about the Gulag, even its supposedly positive aspects of human transformation and economic production, quickly dried up in the mid-1930s as the secret police adopted a new culture of secrecy. The Gulag's size, the locations of its camps, and how it operated became closely guarded state secrets.

The expansion of the Gulag continued rapidly through the early to mid-1930s as the number of inmates increased from around 179,000 at the beginning of 1930 to 510,000 by the end of 1933. In late 1931 and early 1932, the infamous Dalstroy camp complex in the far northeastern corner of Russia was created to mine gold. Inmates built the city of Magadan and dozens of smaller settlements, along with roads, bridges, farms, and other infrastructure to support mining operations. Simultaneously, the Gulag established another large camp in the coal-rich Pechora Basin in northern Siberia, where the city of Vorkuta and other settlements were built by inmate labor. By late 1932 these two camps would each hold more than 10,000 prisoners. Others were sent to construct the Baikal-Amur Mainline, a railway designed to complement the Tran Siberian Railroad in moving goods and people between central Siberia and the Pacific Ocean. And as construction of the White Sea—Baltic Sea Canal concluded, many inmates were dispatched to build a new canal linking the Moscow and Volga Rivers.

These early projects illustrate precisely what the Gulag was to be: a network of large camps devoted to massive public works projects, logging, mining, and large-scale agriculture, tasks the regime considered "of exceptional economic importance." Moreover, most camps were located in sparsely inhabited regions, meaning that inmates were not just laborers but colonists. Indeed, many of them were induced either by job offers or by legal restrictions on movement to remain in the region of their camp after release.[6] Large camps contributing markedly to Stalin's project of rapid industrialization while also serving to colonize vast sections of the Eurasian landmass made the Gulag distinct among contemporary penal systems. Yet this was not predetermined by the Bolshevik Revolution of 1917. Inmates could have been held in local facilities and tasked with various jobs in their own home provinces. Indeed, this is what happened in the corrective-labor colonies for short-term inmates (to be discussed shortly). But Stalin and his trusted advisers calculated that transporting equal numbers of free laborers plus their families to northern Siberia and other remote regions would be prohibitively complicated and expensive. Prisoners, they decided, were the logical choice for such tasks.

This matter raises an important question of intentionalism with which scholars have long grappled. Some have conjectured that Stalin and the secret police imprisoned people explicitly for their usefulness as forced laborers. This line of thinking seems to make sense, given what we have just discussed. But when the Soviet archives were opened in the 1990s, little evidence was found to support such a conclusion. Arrests were made to cleanse socialist society of those who committed crimes or who were deemed enemies of socialism. (A secondary calculation for arrests made by individual policemen was that more arrests proved their loyalty and usefulness.) Nowhere do we find the country's political leadership or even secret police leadership calling for arrests in order to provide more laborers for gold production or canal construction. It is possible that such thinking existed, but the available evidence strongly suggests that although Stalin and the secret police eagerly used the labor of convicts in the interests of building the Soviet economy, mass repression was not driven by economic demands.[7]

Even if inmates were not arrested for their economic value, the centrality of labor to Gulag operations is undeniable. To revisit a question already posed, memoirists and historians alike have asked whether the Gulag was primarily a political institution built to punish enemies or an economic institution designed to employ unfree labor for the benefit of the state. Or was it, as the Soviet state itself proclaimed, a penal system designed to re-educate wayward citizens? These pressures, inherited from the 1920s and even from prerevolutionary Russia, were on stark display in the Gulag.[8] But one thing united these competing tasks of production, punishment, and re-education: labor. Labor benefitted the state, a state that aspired to create an industrial socialist economy that would outpace the capitalist West. Labor in theory served to re-educate prisoners, particularly when accompanied by propaganda teaching them of its societal importance. This was supposed to be labor "which transforms people from nonexistence and insignificance into heroes," as chief prosecutor Andrey Vyshinsky put it.[9] Finally, labor was used to punish. It was forced labor, after all, designed to be longer and harder than labor performed by "free" Soviet citizens.

All three aims—production, re-education, and punishment—were present in the camps of the Stalin-era Gulag. But the lived experience of both prisoners and their jailers confirm that production concerns were almost always paramount. As one camp administrator remembered, his superior officers "constantly cursed at us and threatened to slam us into prison" unless all prisoners worked and fulfilled their set norms.[10] It should not be surprising, therefore, to learn that Gulag officials often referred to their inmates as "labor power," the "work contingent," or just "the contingent," bureaucratic terms of industrial production rather than correctional terms of a progressive prison system.[11]

This view of inmates primarily as forced laborers rather than wayward citizens in need of correction is illustrated by a couple of surprising practices. First, many inmates were "de-convoyed," meaning they went to work outside the camp without armed escort. This gave Gulag commanders flexibility in labor organization, allowing them to send inmates to acquire supplies, deliver goods, or engage in exploratory expeditions without needing to assign guards to them. In fact, many camp commanders used this practice more than allowed by regulations (by allowing "counterrevolutionary" prisoners to be de-convoyed, for example). In Vorkuta in the early 1940s, one-third of all inmates were de-convoyed as a "production necessity" or less commonly as a privilege to reward good behavior.[12] Several years later, around 11 percent of all Gulag inmates worked without guard supervision.[13] Even more surprisingly, not all inmates lived behind walls and barbed wire; many were given permission to live outside the camp zone and to move freely between the camp, their residences, and their designated worksite. These practices were all about economic efficiency and directly contradicted the principles of isolation and punishment.

A similar practice illustrating the primacy of production was the creation of *sharashkas*, special camps where some of the USSR's top technical specialists were held. Arrested for perceived disloyalty to the

Soviet regime, these incarcerated engineers and scientists perfected mining processes and designed military aircraft, radios, artillery shells, and industrial equipment. To stimulate their intellectual labor, living and working conditions were much better than regular Gulag camps.[14] *Sharashka* inmates were also granted early release at higher rates than ordinary prisoners, perhaps as a reward for their service and also so that they could continue their work as "free" citizens in a more productive environment.

Corrective-Labor Colonies

Though the Gulag expanded rapidly in the early 1930s, it did not hold all of the Soviet Union's inmates. Prisoners with sentences of three years or less continued to be sent to houses of correction that were in every province and thus did not require lengthy and resource-intensive transfers to Siberia, Central Asia, or the Far North. These were operated not by the secret police but by the People's Commissariat of Justice, which in 1930 renamed them "corrective-labor colonies," a linguistic parallel to the Gulag's "corrective-labor camps." Most were small, but, true to the spirit of the decade, a large corrective-labor colony was established in the booming industrial city of Magnitogorsk, with inmates sent from around the USSR. Living conditions were poor and many escaped due to a lack of barbed wire and guards. As for labor and re-education, the prisoners were "not deprived of the opportunity to take part in the great construction of the USSR," as the colony newspaper declared, and were put to work building the city and its famous steel mills.[15] As in the Gulag, labor in the corrective-labor colonies became central, both as a way of measuring an inmate's supposed level of re-education and as a way of making colonies financially self-supporting.

Production mandates during this era of rapid industrialization quickly led to tension between the OGPU and the Commissariat of Justice, with the former accusing the latter of improperly keeping the strongest and healthiest inmates for itself and the Commissariat of Justice accusing the OGPU of refusing to accept old and disabled prisoners. The agencies clearly understood that Stalin was impressed not by inmate re-education but by making the greatest contribution to the national economy. This conclusion was only rarely questioned. As one Commissariat of Justice official, in a moment of ironic reflection concerning the aims of the Soviet penal system mused, "if it is so profitable to have inmates, why should we try to reduce the number?"[16]

Ultimately, this dual system did not last long. Stalin favored the secret police and in 1934 the Gulag was given the country's corrective-labor colonies with their 200,000 inmates. In requesting this consolidation, secret police boss Genrikh Yagoda remarked that "the OGPU camps are experiencing a colossal shortfall of laborers in all projects under their supervision ... The transfer of short-term prisoners [from the Ministry of Justice] to the OGPU camps would partly alleviate this gap."[17] All prisoners, regardless of their sentence or who sentenced them, would now be under the Gulag's jurisdiction and sent to wherever their labor was most needed. Establishing the Gulag as a unified system of corrective-labor camps and corrective-labor colonies under the secret police's jurisdiction ended the bureaucratic infighting over the country's prisoners that had lasted from 1917 to 1934. And this consolidated system would, in essence, endure until the collapse of the Soviet Union.

Execution and Other Punishments

Not everyone branded as an enemy of the Soviet regime in the 1930s was sentenced to incarceration. Many were deemed irredeemable and thus unworthy of further existence in a socialist society, even as forced laborers. During the collectivization drive of the late 1920s and early 1930s, for instance, Soviet propaganda declared the "liquidation of the *kulaks* as a class." *Kulak* was a pejorative term for rich peasants that was applied to opponents of collectivization and other supposed troublemakers in the villages; some 30,000 of them were executed. The legal justification for this was to classify ordinary crimes as political ones—stealing from collective farms or harassing state officials could now qualify as grave political crimes and the death penalty could thus be applied. Many judges were unhappy with this and continued to give out lenient sanctions, but most ultimately buckled under pressure from Communist Party leaders who demanded harsh sentences, including execution. This policy of politicizing ordinary crimes in order to hand out death sentences or long terms of imprisonment quickly became a central feature of Stalinist justice in the 1930s.

As Gulag sentences grew longer and executions increased, judges handed out fewer forms of other punishment. But there was one important exception: the secret police in the 1930s, in addition to the Gulag, also ran the Soviet Union's vast system of so-called special settlements. In 1930–31, almost two million people—primarily *kulaks* and their families—were exiled indefinitely to these settlements which, like Gulag camps, were typically located in remote and inhospitable corners of the Soviet Union. These settlements were also tasked with similar aims to those of the Gulag: isolation from society, financial self-sufficiency, contribution to the national economy, and re-education through labor. Special settlers were considered less dangerous than Gulag inmates, but they too were supposed to become honest, hardworking Soviet citizens as well as productive settlers in the vast remote landscapes of Soviet Eurasia. That settlers were not convicted of crimes and were rather targeted as hostile civilians make the special settlements similar in important ways to colonial-era concentration camps.

Even more than the haphazardly organized Gulag camps, the special settlements were created without any master plan, with settlers sent to a particular region often with little more than the clothes on their backs. Local officials, given late notice of their coming and with few resources to help with their accommodation, had to figure out how to feed them and where to settle them (often, ultimately, in dense forests and other uninhabited areas). The process, in other words, was marked by bureaucratic confusion in Moscow and starvation in the settlements in the first three years of their existence.[18] As one former settler numbly recalled the death of her parents, "There wasn't enough for them to eat. They got sick and died."[19]

Most special settlers were eventually put to work cutting timber, though others labored on construction sites or on large-scale farms.

Here, as in the Gulag, hours were long and plan fulfillment took precedence over the health or re-education of the settlers.[20] There were typically no guards at the special settlements, but leaving the settlement or associated worksite was prohibited and harshly punished. Still, escapes were common in the first few years—over 70,000 in 1930 alone—until living conditions were normalized to some extent. And even though some settlers became eligible for return to their native villages through hard labor, the secret police received Stalin's approval to keep them indefinitely. For the purposes of colonizing the country, exile to a special settlement was made permanent.

Similar to the special settlements, the OGPU in late 1932 also created a "grandiose plan" of "labor villages" slated to hold 2 million exiled prisoners (soon reduced to 1 million, then half a million) in Siberia and Kazakhstan. This was designed for *kulaks* who had escaped the repression of 1930–31, along with several other categories of suspected enemies of Soviet power, including peasants living without permission in the cities and short-term prisoners sentenced by the OGPU. This new project, however, which was designed to potentially replace the Gulag camps, was poorly managed, and local officials vehemently opposed the transfer of such labor settlers to their regions. In the most infamous example, several thousand people culled from the country's cities were dumped on the Nazino island in the Ob River. Guards treated them sadistically and the absence of supplies soon resulted in fighting for resources, isolated cases of cannibalism, and death by starvation of thousands of people. Such an outcome illustrates the deep and violent paradoxes of a regime bent on creating an industrial socialist society that too often produced death and destruction.[21] The Nazino affair, as it was called during a lengthy investigation, ultimately discredited the system of labor villages and the scheme was abandoned.

A final type of mass exile that occurred during the 1930s involved ethnic minorities who lived close to the Soviet Union's borders and were suspected of potential disloyalty. Soviet Poles, for instance, were thought susceptible to collusion with neighboring Poland, which could ultimately lead to capitalist military intervention, something Soviet leaders intensely feared in the paranoid culture of the 1930s.

Thousands of Poles were exiled away from the Polish border during the early 1930s; tens of thousands of Ukrainians, Poles, and Germans were then deported in a second round of ethnic cleansing to prevent the region from being turned into "a bridgehead for an attack on Soviet Ukraine."[22] Some were sent only to Eastern Ukraine, but many others were relocated to Central Asia. Tens of thousands of Finns and other ethnic minorities were then removed from the Leningrad border region and sent to Siberia and Central Asia.

The largest of these deportations occurred in 1937, when the secret police rounded up virtually all Koreans—some 172,000 of them—living in the eastern borderland provinces of the Soviet Union and forcibly exiled them to Central Asia. The ostensible justification for this was security concerns with neighboring Japan, which exerted imperial control over Korea and Manchuria. As secret police boss Nikolay Yezhov wrote to Stalin in 1937 in a blatantly false accusation, "These Koreans are without a doubt cadres of Japanese espionage."[23] Relocated to Kazakhstan and Uzbekistan, Soviet Koreans faced poor living conditions, forced labor mobilization, and various legal disabilities due solely to their ethnicity, something expressly forbidden by the Soviet constitution. They were not placed in camps surrounded by barbed wire, nor were they categorized as "special settlers," but they were kept in specific regions, mostly concentrated on collective farms, and monitored by the secret police (which was renamed, confusingly, the People's Commissariat of Internal Affairs, or NKVD, in 1934—note that this is a different agency from the NKVD of the 1920s). And many died during or after the deportation from malnutrition and disease. These large-scale deportations of ethnic minority groups in the 1930s, as we will see in Chapter 4, provided a model that would be repeated during the 1940s.

The Great Terror and the Gulag on the Eve of War

In December 1934, a top Communist Party official, Sergei Kirov, was shot and killed. Some have blamed Stalin for the murder, suggesting that Stalin envied Kirov's popularity in the Communist Party, but the evidence remains inconclusive. In any event, the murder set in motion a series of ever-wider investigations, trials, and judicial reforms that played out over the following years. Notably, Stalin made it easier to convict people of counterrevolutionary crimes and eliminated the possibility of appeal for such crimes. In July 1936, a public show trial was held in which two of Stalin's opponents from the succession struggle of the 1920s, along with fourteen other defendants, were found guilty and executed for conspiring with Leon Trotsky to kill Kirov. But this trial did not put an end to the paranoid search for political opponents and other "enemies of the people" who, in Stalin's mind, threatened the construction of socialism in the USSR and the country's ability to defend itself against foreign invaders. The Soviet Union was already involved in the Spanish Civil War and Stalin feared that war with Nazi Germany was likely.

Ultimately, the result of the Kirov investigations and the paranoid atmosphere of the 1930s was the Great Terror of 1937–38. The secret police under Genrikh Yagoda and then his successor, Nikolay Yezhov, targeted a wide range of people, accusing them of being "terrorists," "spies," "counterrevolutionaries," and "anti-Soviet elements." Among those arrested were intellectuals, cultural elites, Communist Party functionaries, diplomats, factory bosses, army officers, collective farm managers, priests, and people with prior criminal records. Even the secret police itself was thoroughly purged. Around 1.6 million people endured arrest, interrogation, and speedy trial, often by extrajudicial bodies called *troikas*, with the secret police falsifying evidence and extracting confessions through threats and torture. This was all directed by Stalin and his top lieutenants, but it was also marked by "excesses" by local officials that Moscow largely ignored or even encouraged until late in the campaign. In the end, around half of those arrested were executed and most of the rest were sent to the Gulag.

The Great Terror affected the camps and colonies of the Gulag in several ways. First, existing inmates were subjected to arrest, investigation, trial, and a new sentence, often for the same alleged crime for which they were originally sentenced. In 1938, for instance, the camp leadership of Dalstroy handed out 12,566 new sentences, including 5,866 executions, which it summarily carried out.[24] In the Pechora Basin, around 2,500 were executed. Being already imprisoned in the Gulag, in other words, did not save people from the Terror; they too were arrested and executed in mass numbers. And it was not just prisoners: Gulag commanders and other personnel were also arrested and executed. Matvey Berman, head of the Gulag for much of the 1930s, was himself accused of leading a "Right-Trotskyist terrorist and sabotage organization" and executed.[25]

Second, despite tens of thousands of executions in the Gulag, the Terror quickly and substantially increased the overall number of inmates. Official reports show just over 800,000 corrective-labor camp inmates in early 1937 and over 1.3 million by the end of 1938 (with hundreds of thousands more in corrective-labor colonies and prisons). Already an institution of mass incarceration, the Gulag now dwarfed the Soviet penal institutions of the 1920s and every other penal system around the world at the time, including the concentration camp system of Germany prior to the Second World War. Over 1 percent of the Soviet population was behind bars or barbed wire, with around another percent in various forms of exile.

This dramatic and sudden increase in prisoners resulted in the haphazard creation of new camps during the winter of 1937–38 and a terrible deterioration of living conditions due to overcrowding. As one of the architects of the Terror, Procurator General Andrey Vyshinsky, observed in an unintentionally ironic report to secret police boss Yezhov in early 1938, the condition of many prisoners was "absolutely intolerable." Starvation rations, lack of clothing and bedding, rampant disease, and inmates living in tents during the brutal winter with no heat defined Gulag life. Some prisoners, Vyshinsky said, "have deteriorated to the point of losing any resemblance to human beings." One of Vyshinsky's inspecting procurators reported that "hundreds of telegrams sent to the Gulag about the catastrophic situation in the camp go unanswered. People become brutalized, and some are nearly insane …. but new prisoners keep coming and coming."[26] A similar report from the Pechora Basin spoke of camp units becoming "havens of infectious disease and mass death."[27]

Significantly, a majority of those imprisoned during the Great Terror were accused of espionage, conspiracy, or terrorism against the Soviet regime. The vast majority, as teams of Soviet judicial investigators would "discover" after Stalin's death, were innocent of any crime. This large number of citizens sent to the Gulag in extrajudicial fashion for perceived disloyalty or untrustworthiness make the Gulag, at least in part, a concentration camp system. Similar to Western concentration camps in the colonial setting or in Nazi Germany before the outbreak of the Second World War, the Gulag held suspect civilians during a time of heightened social mobilization or war. This idea of the Gulag as a network of concentration camps during and after the Great Terror is also supported to some extent by camp operations. Political prisoners endured a climate of vastly increased suspicion and abuse from guards and administrators, steeped in the dehumanizing rhetoric used in the Soviet press. The country was preparing for war, the narrative went, and had to cleanse itself of internal enemies. Emboldened by these attacks, guards verbally and physically abused political prisoners. Those convicted of political crimes were also removed from "light" work assignments, which they had often been given because of their unique skills, and instead assigned to hard physical labor. At least in relation to political prisoners, the aim of retribution during this era often took priority over re-education and even production.

After more than a year and a half of terror, Stalin in late 1938 arrested Nikolay Yezhov and placed Lavrenty Beria in charge of the secret police. Mass arrests ceased and some semblance of normality returned to the country. In relation to the Gulag, Stalin instructed Beria to restore the economic production disrupted by the Terror. In response, Beria eliminated early release by parole and the similar system of workday credits for labor fulfillment. He prioritized construction projects valued by Stalin and increased the use of *sharashkas* for imprisoned scientists and engineers. He improved food rations and clothing allotments for prisoners but simultaneously increased penalties for inmates who refused to work or broke camp regulations. Living conditions on average improved somewhat, though inspection reports continued to highlight the plight of mass numbers of sick and emaciated prisoners. In fact, Beria's focus on some economic projects meant that non-prioritized camps saw their living conditions deteriorate.[28] In any case, the utter disregard for the lives and health of Gulag prisoners was a lasting legacy of the Stalinist 1930s and of the Great Terror in particular.

Conclusions

With around a million inmates by the end of the 1930s, not to mention another million detained in special settlements and hundreds of thousands in exile, the Soviet Gulag on the eve of the Second World War was a massive institution. A vast and somewhat haphazardly organized network of corrective-labor camps, corrective-labor colonies, and prisons, it spread across the Soviet Union but was most prominent in sparsely settled regions such as the Far North, the Urals, Siberia, the Far East, and Kazakhstan. Run by the secret police, the Gulag was tasked with: (1) isolating those sentenced to deprivation of liberty, (2) forcing them to work for the benefit of the state, and (3) re-educating them into honest Soviet citizens. But Gulag operations overwhelmingly favored economic production out of these three aims, and the unstated aim of inflicting retributive punishment also competed as an institutional priority. As part of the Soviet repressive apparatus, the Gulag flourished in this decade of social engineering, upheaval, famine, and violence. And though it certainly exemplified the chaos and brutality of Stalin's regime, it also embodied to some extent the hopes and dreams of the socialist project. As historian Steven Barnes writes of the Gulag's contradictions, "Exploitation, oppression, and mass death coexisted with reeducation, redemption, and mass release."[29] Such themes would prove to be an enduring legacy of the Stalinist system.

CHAPTER 3
EVERYDAY LIFE IN STALIN'S CAMPS

It is one thing to understand the Gulag as an institution, part of the ambitious Soviet project to build socialism. It is another thing to understand the very human experiences of those trapped in this system. The Soviet Union aimed at an orderly, rational penal system that worked toward specific aims, but in actuality, official documents and memoirs reveal a chaotic environment of corruption, deceit, disobedience, theft, beatings, and privation, along with starvation, torture, and murder. Labor was hastily organized, poorly monitored, and potentially dangerous. Camps were often in a primitive state of development, and prisoners faced intense psychological challenges associated with navigating camp society. Yet they also experienced surprising moments of hope, joy, and friendship. In its chaos, the Gulag laid bare the full range of human emotion.

That life in the Gulag was difficult should not be surprising. This was a penal system, after all, that shared with prisons globally the deprivation of liberty, autonomy, security, goods and services, and sexual relations with committed partners.[1] But the Soviet camp experience was certainly worse than the average prison in Europe or North America. Living conditions were more spartan, the food was worse, the guards were more violent, and the hard compulsory labor added an extra element of exhaustion and danger to the lives of most inmates. Life in the Soviet Gulag, in other words, was difficult often to the point of deadliness, and for many who survived, the physical and psychological scars would never fully heal.

Getting to the Gulag

Arrest, interrogation, and sentencing were traumatic first steps that led to imprisonment in one of the camps or colonies of the Gulag. Memoirists recall in vivid detail their first days in prison as they endured confinement, deprivation, and psychological (and for many physical) pressure to confess to a crime. Here they learned their first lessons of life behind bars—whom to trust, how to circumvent regulations, how to hide prized possessions during searches, and how to endure both suffering and boredom. This pre-sentencing phase of their imprisonment could last weeks or months. And though convinced of their innocence—"this is a mistake," said Jacques Rossi to his interrogators—many confessed under duress to crimes not committed.[2] But even if they did not, conviction and a multiyear sentence was the typical result. For some this came as an intense psychological shock. For others, there was a sense of relief that at least their fate was now known, their interrogations over.

After sentencing, inmates were slated for transfer to a corrective-labor institution. This typically involved a torturously long railway journey in a cattle car crammed with other inmates. Little food or water was provided, the heat was often unbearable, and illness quickly spread. For some inmates the train journey led not to a camp but to a port where they were then loaded onto a ship. For those sent to the Kolyma gold fields, the passage north through the Sea of Okhotsk was nightmarish. Sea sickness combined with disease produced an endless stream of vomit and diarrhea that the ship's few toilets could not handle. Overcrowding and a lack of proper guarding resulted in sleep deprivation, rampant theft, and gang rape. "Anyone who has seen Dante's hell would say that it was nothing beside what went on in that ship," one inmate recalled.[3] On both trains and ships, many inmates died; others spent significant time in the camp hospital after arrival.

Those who survived transportation to their camp were brought to headquarters. Here they showered, had their heads and pubic areas shaved to prevent the spread of lice, and sorted. Memoirists recall how they were lined up naked and inspected by medical personnel (for muscle tone, obvious sores or injuries, rotten teeth, etc.), and then assigned to one of the various "camp points" according to their health and labor capability. The final leg of their journey then ensued as they were marched to the camp point where they would spend the next several months or perhaps years of their lives. Most prisoners spent time in several different camp points during their time behind barbed wire. And while these often differed dramatically in terms of living conditions, labor, and social life, I will try to give in the pages that follow a sense of what life was like in the Stalin-era Gulag.

The Daily Routine and Basic Living Conditions

The typical day for Gulag inmates started at four or five o'clock in the morning when they were awakened in their communal barracks by a guard or inmate orderly. The barracks were usually of simple wooden construction, though some were brick and others were large canvas tents, railway cars, or earthen dugouts. Dozens or even hundreds of inmates inhabited each barrack, which were frequently overcrowded (note that the tablecloth and flowers seen in Figure 3.1 would have been placed there only for this photograph to make the living space seem more pleasant) [Figure 3.1]. Most barracks were poorly heated in the winter, with bunks by the wood-burning stove fought for while those closest to the door were left for inmates on the bottom of the social hierarchy. As one memoirist related of the cold, "A few times I … woke up in the morning to find that my headscarf and hair had frozen to the plywood wall of the barrack."[4] Or as a guard candidly recorded in his diary, "There are bare bunks, gaps everywhere in the walls, snow on the sleeping prisoners, no firewood. A mass of shivering people, intelligent, educated people."[5]

After arising from their bunks, getting dressed, and perhaps relieving themselves in an indoor bucket or outdoor latrine, the inmates filed outside to the camp courtyard. There they were counted and given a few words of instruction, rebuke, or inspiration from a camp officer. As Kazimierz Zarod related of the counting, "the guards often made mistakes, and then there had to

Figure 3.1 Vorkuta prison barracks, 1945.

be a second count. On a morning when it was snowing this was a long, cold, agonizing process."[6] The prisoners then filed off to the dining hall for breakfast, often consisting of bread and thin soup or cooked buckwheat or barley. Bowls and utensils—mostly wood but sometimes tin—were scarce and therefore closely guarded possessions. After breakfast, the majority of prisoners were marched off to work. The working day was officially nine or ten hours, but in practice it often lasted longer—one consistently finds in memoirs and official inspection reports accounts of twelve- or even fourteen-hour workdays. Prisoners were given a short break for lunch at the worksite, which typically consisted of little more than the bread they had been issued at breakfast.

After the work shift was completed, the inmates were marched back to the camp courtyard and counted again. They would then be served dinner, typically bread and a thin soup, after which they would attend to various preparations for the next day, such as hanging wet clothes up to dry or mending tools. Finally, at least on some days, they might have an hour or so before lights out for reading, talking, playing chess (permitted) or card games (not permitted), or perhaps attending a camp-sponsored cultural event or educational class. More frequently, they would collapse, exhausted on their bunk until early morning the next day. Like all prison regimens, the daily routine for Gulag prisoners often became monotonous. Rest days were provided every seven or ten days, giving inmates a chance to write letters, wash clothes, clean the barracks, attend cultural productions, get haircuts, and shower. But in periods of intense production pressure, days off could be cancelled.

The daily regimen was enforced by a lengthy list of regulations detailing expectations and prohibitions. Good behavior could be rewarded by official commendations, increased rations, privileged work assignments, and various forms of early release. Violations could earn a warning, reduced rations, and time in the penalty isolator (solitary confinement). However, prisoners often found themselves punished for things other than deviations from the stated regulations. As Aleksandr Solzhenitsyn described,

> What was the [penalty isolator] given for? For whatever they felt like: You didn't please your chief; you didn't say hello the way you should have; you didn't get up on time; you didn't go to bed on time; you were late for roll call; you took the wrong path; you were wrongly dressed; you smoked where it was forbidden; you kept extra things in your barracks ...[7]

Like the daily routine, such regulations and the capriciousness of punishment would be familiar to many inmates the world over. Yet in the Gulag, there was often an extra measure of vindictive punishment meted out against those who got on the wrong side of the guards.

Labor

Labor occupied most of Gulag inmates' waking hours. It was the defining feature of their existence. As Solzhenitsyn described it, "the life of the [prisoners] consists of work, work, work; of starvation, cold, and cunning."[8] Inmates worked as welders, drivers, bricklayers, lathe operators, mechanics, farmers, miners, loaders, diggers, sewing-machine operators, blacksmiths, medical orderlies, cooks, accountants, agronomists, surveyors, cowherds, lumberjacks, librarians, actors, maids, couriers, electricians, and a hundred other positions. Some prisoners were even put to work guarding their fellow inmates. As Solzhenitsyn sarcastically noted, "it is indeed much easier to enumerate the occupations the prisoners never did have: the manufacture of sausages and confectionary goods."[9]

Labor demands were relentless, with intense pressure placed on camp administrators and guards to fulfil the production plan. Faced with the possibility of punishment (lower wages, demotion, or even arrest) for non-fulfillment of the plan, camp bosses worked their prisoners hard. Long hours in any weather conditions was the norm. Although Gulag regulations prohibited labor when the mercury dipped below negative forty degrees, prisoners were often forced to work in such conditions anyway.[10] In the summertime they suffered from heat, gnats, and mosquitos. As one inmate recalled, the mosquitos "filled up your eyes, your nose and throat, and the taste of them was sweet, like blood. The more you moved and waved them away, the more they attacked."[11] In any weather conditions, work-related accidents due to exhaustion and inadequate safety precautions were common.

Many inmates found their daily labor quotas difficult or impossible to attain. Particularly for those unaccustomed to hard labor, chopping down a certain number of trees or excavating rocky soil by shovel could feel hopeless. As the university professor Eugenia Ginzburg described of her time felling trees in Kolyma, "for three days Galya and I struggled to do the impossible. Poor trees—how they must have suffered at being mangled by our inexpert hands!"[12] But as Ginzburg quickly discovered, Gulag inmates routinely engaged in deceitful practices, known in the camps as *tufta*. Sawing the ends off an old pile of logs to make it look like they were freshly cut was one such way to simulate plan fulfillment. Pilfering already mined ore from a stockpile to then present it as new production was another. Or inmates could simply bribe (or threaten) guards and camp accountants to falsify production records. Even camp authorities falsified numbers to protect themselves from disciplinary action for not meeting production goals. As one former administrator recalled, for two weeks he had prisoners work on camp improvements rather than production while "feeding the leadership 'tufta' ... that would show all the prisoners fulfilling the daily plan by 100 percent."[13]

Camp authorities had various tools at their disposal to stimulate production. Written and oral propaganda shamed "slackers," such as in the mock graveyard in Figure 3.2. Here the names of underperforming inmates along with their level of plan fulfillment are given against a mock grave, suggesting that the lazy will perish. Other propaganda praised those who fulfilled labor norms and reminded inmates of the global importance of their work as the Soviet Union waged a war of ideas against the capitalist West. "Labor competitions" were organized

Figure 3.2 Mock graveyard of underproducing Gulag inmates, 1933.

between brigades, with rewards granted in the form of extra rations or other goods from the camp store. Other programs provided for early release. From the very beginning of the Gulag system, parole and work-related amnesties were promised to exceptional workers. Starting in 1931, inmates could also earn workday credits that reduced the length of their sentence by up to one-third if production goals were met (this program was abolished in the aftermath of the Great Terror but then restored in the 1950s).

One of the most powerful tools for stimulating production was tying rations to plan fulfillment. As one fellow inmate bluntly told Janusz Bardach, "You work, you eat. You stop working, you die."[14] Or as a camp boss told a group of new arrivals, "This isn't a seaside resort! You've got your norm to fulfill, and you'll be fed according to output."[15] Those who produced 70 percent of the daily plan were given just 70 percent of their daily ration. This could quickly have predictable consequences. As deputy Gulag boss Semyon Firin in 1933 frankly remarked, "It often happens in the camps that a weak, emaciated prisoner is given a regular work task. By systematically failing to do his job, he receives a smaller ration of food, and, therefore, instead of recuperating, he becomes still weaker."[16] Yet those who worked hard to exceed the work assignment and were given proportional rations that exceeded the daily norm could also die of malnutrition, with their caloric expenditure exceeding their intake.[17]

For many labor tasks, assignments were made not to individual prisoners but to brigades of inmates who bore collective responsibility for plan fulfillment. In theory, this created a system of peer pressure to ensure high productivity—no prisoner would want to be responsible for the brigade not receiving its full ration. Such a system also made it possible for stronger prisoners to cover for weaker prisoners, and many inmates write of this being the norm with newly arrived inmates or those just out of the penalty isolator— they were given a few days of cover by the brigade as they adjusted to the pace of production. As one inmate recalled of a fair and caring brigade leader, "everyone who got into his brigade considered himself lucky, and was saved from death."[18] Ultimately, a persistent source of conflict in the Gulag was between brigade leaders, who sought the best workers, and among brigade members accusing each other of not carrying their weight.

Violence

In addition to relentless labor demands, Gulag camps were rife with violence and dehumanization. "At every step," one inmate recalled, "they tried to make it clear to us that we weren't people."[19] Part of this was tied to the productive rationale of the camps, where inmates were seen as little more than manpower. But part was tied to the ideologies of class conflict and capitalist encirclement that framed many Soviet subjects as "enemies of the people." Guards and other Gulag officials came from all walks and philosophies of life—most were not sadists bent on inflicting self-gratifying violence. As former inmate Lev Razgon described, "among them were both the clever and the stupid, good and evil men, bureaucrats and the fanatics."[20] But regardless of their background or emotional predispositions, they were taught to fear prisoners and see them as parasites and enemies. It is therefore not surprising that although regulations disallowed beatings and other forms of guard-on-inmate abuse, such occurrences were commonplace. One report from the Krasnoyarsk Camp in 1939, for instance, found that inmates were shot, beaten with a variety of instruments (sticks, axes, shovels, rifle butts, boots, etc.), forced to eat dirt, bitten by guard dogs, and stripped naked and exposed to either freezing temperatures or mosquitos.[21] Guards were occasionally punished for such violations, but more often they were ignored or even encouraged by superior officers.

The most serious violation of camp discipline was escape. Escape was relatively common in the early to mid-1930s but became increasingly difficult as additional guards, barbed wire, and watchtowers created more secure camp environments. Those who attempted escape and were caught were typically beaten, charged with a crime, and given a new sentence. Sometimes, however, they were killed after capture, with the official report on the matter falsely claiming they were shot during the escape attempt or pursuit. As one inmate later recalled, "if they caught you running away, they killed you, everyone knew that. And before they killed you, what's more, they beat you savagely."[22] One guard in his diary justified such violence: "Before I am even out of bed, another escape. I'll have to go looking for him tomorrow. We should just shoot three in each phalanx to put them off the idea. Escape disrupts everything."[23]

Of course, violence at times went the other way, with inmates beating or killing Gulag officials, sometimes during escape attempts. More often, though, inmates inflicted violence against their fellow inmates. Part of this was the struggle for scarce resources, with some robbing others for food or clothes (the gang aspect of this type of violence will be discussed in the next chapter). Violence occurred based on personality clashes that boiled over in the pressure cooker environment of the prison camp. Ethnic conflict also occurred, with Russian prisoners fighting against Central Asians, Ukrainians, and other groups.

A final form of violence experienced by Gulag inmates was sexual assault. Gulag bosses pressured primarily young female inmates into coercive relationships in exchange for better rations, nicer living accommodations, easy labor, or early release. Guards and administrators, fueled by alcohol, lust, and a desire to assert dominance over the bodies of prisoners, violently raped female (and occasionally male) inmates. Rape perpetrated by inmates was also not uncommon. Though difficult due to Gulag policies that segregated prisoners by gender, it occurred where jobsites featured mixed groups of inmates and when male prisoners were allowed into female zones (for a work assignment or through bribery). Male-on-male rape was also common among prisoners. As Varlam Shalamov related, "almost all the professional criminals were homosexuals. When no women were at hand, they seduced and infected other men—most frequently by threatening them with a knife, less frequently in exchange for 'rags' or 'bread.'"[24] Rape perpetrated by female inmates also occurred but seems to have existed primarily in the fertile imaginations of male inmates, who relished sharing exaggerated tales of such incidents.

Typically covered up by authorities and often not discussed in memoirs due to its shameful nature, rape in the Gulag remains an evasive subject of research.

Clothing, Food, and Medicine

Along with strict regulations, backbreaking labor, and violence, inmates suffered from poor living conditions associated with clothing, food, and medicine. Most inmates arrived with little more than the clothes on their backs. Camps were supposed to issue clothing appropriate for the climate and labor, but this was always in short supply. Rain gear and winter boots were difficult to find, and coats, pants, shirts, gloves, hats, and undergarments tended to be in poor condition. Inmates often constructed homemade needles (prohibited according to regulations) to mend their clothes, and they bartered or stole from other inmates as the opportunities arose. Unsurprisingly, frostbite and hypothermia were common occurrences. As Polina Benoni recalled of her thin footwear in winter working conditions, "The shoes grew hard and froze to my foot wraps, and the foot wraps froze to my feet …. All that night, my feet were in agony and burning. By morning, huge purple blisters appeared, and I went to work with feet like that."[25]

Another common complaint was that rations were almost always insufficient and of poor nutritional quality. Soup was little more than flavored water. Potatoes were often rotten. Flour for making bread could be adulterated with sawdust or other material. Meat and dairy products in the camp were rare, as were fresh fruit and vegetables. As Eugenia Ginzburg recalled of her time in a Gulag prison, the amount of food was "enough to keep one actually from starving to death, but the quality was such that one could scarcely manage to live on it, either. There were no vitamins in the food."[26] After transfer to a camp, Ginzburg found that the quantity, tied to labor output, could quickly lead to starvation: "After receiving the morsel of bread corresponding to our 'output,' we were led out next day to our place of work, literally staggering from weakness."[27] Scurvy (caused by vitamin C deficiency), pellagra (caused by niacin deficiency), dystrophy, and other diseases associated with malnutrition ravaged Gulag camps. Many inmates recalled the barely living "goners," roaming around the camp with no energy and no hope for recovery, scrounging for any scrap of food to put off death for one more day. Others became vicious because of the persistent hunger. "Even smart, cultured people," one political prisoner recalled, "became animals."[28]

For those suffering from disease, medical attention was not guaranteed. Gulag guards and medical personnel were on alert for "simulators" looking to get a day off work and rejected all but the most urgent medical requests. Memoirs are replete with stories of faked illness and more disturbing accounts of prisoners ingesting various objects (such as chess pieces), cutting themselves, or performing other acts of self-mutilation in order to gain time in the hospital. As Anatoly Zhigulin described of his own decision to self-harm in pursuit of time off work, "I kept chopping, gradually moving my foot closer and closer ... A few more weak chops and finally ... the ax blade bit hard into my boot .... My soldier saw the whole thing, and in his mind it was purely an accident, a bad swing."[29] Unfortunately, camp medical facilities did not always offer salvation. Medicine was scarce, doctors and nurses were in constant short supply, and prisoners without prior medical experience were often drafted into these positions.[30]

Yet camp hospitals frequently did provide respite from hard labor along with increased rations—the two things most sick and exhausted prisoners needed. As Zhigulin related, "Oh, those wonderful ten or twenty days in the hospital! Food for the patients was prepared separately and resembled the real thing ... I just lay there; I could rest. It was clean, warm, cozy."[31] The Gulag even established separate camps for inmates disabled because of injury, illness, or emaciation. The results here were mixed: many inmates died in these camps, but others were restored somewhat to health (only to again be transferred to hard labor in a regular camp). As one former inmate recalled of her time in such a camp, "It was a moment to stop and catch our breath that we remembered for a long time. It did not do that much to improve our health, but we did step back from the edge of the grave just a little."[32]

Social and Cultural Life

The Gulag truly was a frightening institution marked by hardship, suffering, and death. Yet one of the remarkable things that I have found in inmates' letters and memoirs is how much they dwell on the positive aspects of their lives in the camps. Certainly, to some extent, the letters reflect a desire to not frighten loved ones, and memoirs often adopt a narrative of triumph over hardship that privileges the good over the bad. Yet it cannot be denied that deep and lasting friendships developed among prisoners; books, games, cultural productions, and sporting events provided diversion and enlightenment; and the natural environment provided a sense of wonder and beauty. Even labor at times could provide a sense of fulfillment. As former prisoner Anatoly Zhigulin remarked, "Sometimes people ask me whether there were ever any good times in the camps, ever a good mood. Of course there were. The soul always seeks joy, yearns for it."[33] Or in the words of famed writer Sergei Dovlatov, "there is beauty even in prison life. And if you only use dark colors you won't get it right."[34] In short, there was light and beauty to be found in the Gulag amidst the stark deprivation.

As bad as camp life could be, many memoirists portray it positively compared to the filthy, overcrowded prisons where they endured months or years of close confinement during interrogation. In the camp, one was not strictly confined to a cell, and inmates relished the ability to go outside, particularly in the summertime. As one inmate related after a long stint in prison, "I stretched out on some dry timbers under a wooden wall warmed by the sun. All around me were birches, pines, and all kinds of birds chirping in different ways."[35] Many memoirists write glowingly of the fresh air, the plant and animal life that surrounded the camp, and the starry night skies, sometimes punctuated by a display of the northern lights. As I have argued elsewhere, "interactions with the natural world served as a source of knowledge, inspiration, and solace, providing means by which inmates could make sense of or, to some degree, lessen the pains of their incarcerated existence."[36]

Some inmates found joy in correspondence with loved ones. As Arseny Formakov expressed in one of many letters exchanged with his wife, "your concern for me is so touching it almost makes me cry." This followed not just letters but a package she sent that included various books and magazines along with, as Formakov described, "two pussy willow branches, which I immediately stuck in water and then placed in the sun on the windowsill."[37] Others used prayer and secret holiday services to help maintain a fulfilling spiritual life. Menachem Begin encountered a Christian doctor who had endured great trials, having been arrested on a false denunciation from his own wife. And yet in the camps he continued to devote himself to God through prayer. "The truth is that I believe in God," he said, "and no one can take my faith away from me."[38] Eugenia Ginzburg likewise recalled a group of Orthodox Christians who prayed and communed together and who refused to work on Easter: "When they got to the forest clearing they made a neat pile of their axes and saws, sat down quietly on the frozen tree stumps and began to sing hymns."[39]

On occasion, inmates enjoyed sports that provided some escape from the monotony, drudgery, or terror of daily life.[40] Some camps had athletic fields where inmates played informal pickup games on their days off, and the "cultural-educational section" at times organized sporting competitions that included races, shot put, discus, long jump, volleyball, and especially soccer. Music could also provide joy. Inmates at some camps marched to work accompanied by brass bands, and various musical ensembles played evening concerts. As Kazimierz Zarod remembered, "some were professionals, others amateur, but together they made quite good music."[41] The upbeat music and industrial lyrics of songs such as "March of the Concrete Workers" were designed to make labor feel heroic and to express the joy of working toward a brighter future.[42] Such explicitly propagandistic productions were not always appreciated by the inmates, but many memoirists recall enjoying evening concerts put on by bands, orchestras, and choirs. Alexander Dolgun remembered with fondness learning to play the guitar and singing both mournful and funny songs with other inmates. As he remembered, "I would turn to my guitar after witnessing a terrible death or an act of brutal violence and wipe the intolerable scenes from my mind."[43]

For some, cultural, artistic, or intellectual stimulation came from more solitary reflections and interactions. Reading books from the camp library, writing poetry, watching the occasional movie, and singing folk songs or prison ballads promoted individual intellectual growth or at least diversion. Some inmates embroidered, carved wooden figurines, or created dyes with which to illustrate their letters home. Famed actors and directors were able to get transferred from "general labor" to work in Gulag theaters, thanks in part to Gulag bosses eager to mix and mingle with the country's cultural elites and to enjoy high culture in the remote backwaters of the penal archipelago. Such patronage provided jailers with personal prestige, a feeling of accomplishment at bringing high culture to the remotest corners of the USSR, and a way to counter the narrative that the Gulag existed only to punish.[44] For inmates, it could provide special housing, better rations and other privileges, and a chance to use their creative talents. As Arseny Formakov told his wife in a letter, directing a drama troupe "gives me certain privileges, which are not insignificant in my current circumstances"[45] [Figure 3.3].

Figure 3.3 Theater performance at the White Sea—Baltic Sea Canal, 1933.

Social life was perhaps the most important way of finding happiness in the Gulag. Camp society typically split into self-organized groups: intellectuals banded together, as did peasants, professional criminals, religious prisoners, and inmates of various ethnic backgrounds. At times these groups were sources of intense friction in the camps, but the emotional bonds forged with other prisoners often became quite strong. "We became like real sisters," one memoirist related, while others talked of their camp friends as their "family."[46] They shared food and bunks, they worked together, they laughed and cried together, and they supported each other both physically and emotionally. One inmate recalled that "friendship helped us endure all these horrors—our readiness to help one another in difficult moments, and the awareness that we were all suffering the same fate."[47] This was particularly true among imprisoned women, but men experienced this as well. As Janusz Bardach related, "Camp friendships were about one thing: trust .... You wanted to know on whom you could rely during the inevitable daily crises."[48]

Beyond friendship, non-coercive sexuality in the camps was more prevalent than one might imagine. For some, malnourishment and exhaustion, often combined with loyalty to a spouse back home, largely extinguished their sex drive while in the camps. But memoirs and official documents attest that many prisoners forged consensual hetero- and homosexual relationships with fellow inmates and "free" workers in the camps. This was forbidden by Gulag regulations, but communal barracks, bathhouses, and jobsites provided the necessary secrecy. These relationships were often built on genuine love and affection that blossomed under the most trying of circumstances. For some, they were rooted in a craving for intimate human touch to counteract the otherwise callous interpersonal relations that too often defined Gulag life. Former inmate Hava Volovich, for instance, recalled that "our need for love, tenderness, caresses was so desperate that it reached a point of insanity."[49] Sex could also be a tool of barter among prisoners or a form of resistance against the repressive Gulag regime.[50]

To this last point of resistance, many memoirists describe a strategy by female inmates of intentionally getting pregnant to obtain additional rations and time off work. In fact, pregnancy from both coerced and uncoerced sex was prevalent enough that most Gulag camps operated a nursery facility for children born to prisoners. Mothers were given limited visitation rights, particularly to breastfeed, but children who reached a certain age were then shipped off to an orphanage if the mother was still imprisoned. Having an infant in the camp could be a source of love and tenderness behind the barbed wire, but tragically, many children in this system died of malnutrition and neglect. As Volovich sorrowfully related of her baby, born in the camp but transferred to a camp orphanage after several months, "my pudgy little angel with the golden curls soon turned into a pale ghost with blue shadows under her eyes and sores all over her lips." She died before her second birthday.[51]

Conclusions

Given the poor living conditions, insufficient food, heavy labor, and violence of the Gulag, I sometimes wonder at how anyone managed to survive. In fact, millions of people died in the camps or shortly after release (I will discuss these numbers in the next chapter). Yet more survived than died—so how did they do it? Some benefitted from short terms of incarceration. Others entered the camps young and healthy, which certainly improved their chances of survival. Some joined a gang, taking food and clothes from other inmates and relying on group protection to save them. Others agreed to be secret informants, trusting camp officials to protect and perhaps release them early if they passed on information about other inmates. Many inmates credited their education or their religious faith with survival, noting that these things helped them keep hope alive. Former writers and professors recited poetry to each other and recalled tales of survival from great works of fiction, while Christians, Muslims, and Jews prayed, recited scriptures, and communed with fellow believers. Other inmates tied their survival to their families, with children, spouses, and parents at home providing a compelling reason to survive until release.[52]

The most important path to survival was avoiding hard labor. Those who were stuck felling trees or mining gold were much more likely to succumb to exhaustion and starvation, or be killed in a jobsite accident, than those playing a tuba in the camp brass band or preparing meals in the camp kitchen. As most inmates were supposed to be engaged in heavy labor, this strategy was not easily accomplished. But leveraging one's talents or connections to be appointed a medical orderly, cultural worker, or bookkeeper vastly improved one's survival odds. Yet even for those who managed to adopt one or more of these strategies, death could still strike. Luck, it seems, also played a pivotal role in deciding who survived and who died.

CHAPTER 4
THE SECOND WORLD WAR AND THE ZENITH OF THE GULAG SYSTEM

The German invasion of 1941 initiated a four-year war of attrition between the leading proponents of fascism and Marxism: Adolf Hitler's Third Reich and Stalin's Soviet Union. The Second World War was an ideological and, for Hitler, a racial struggle that culminated in tens of millions of deaths and unimaginable destruction. Not surprisingly, this was a time of deep suffering and high mortality for Gulag inmates. As German forces occupied the USSR's best grain-producing regions and Stalin moved the Soviet economy to a wartime footing, privation, overexertion, and starvation resulted. Gulag officials trumpeted their contributions to the successful war effort while actively disguising the mass deaths happening in their labor camps. This was the most perilous time to be a Gulag inmate.

After the victorious conclusion of the war, Soviet imperial expansion meant the export of Soviet penal philosophy and the establishment of Gulag-like penal institutions across the East Bloc. In the Soviet Union itself, recovery from the war was long and difficult. Over 20 million Soviet subjects had died, and countless towns, farms, schools, and other institutions were destroyed. But even while Stalin pursued a policy of wartime reconstruction, he launched new waves of repression that brought the Gulag to its numerical zenith, with over 5 million people imprisoned or in forced internal exile by the early 1950s. For prisoners in the postwar era, labor demands remained high, food was scarce due to the famine of 1946–48, and overcrowding brought difficult living conditions. The postwar Gulag was also a time of increased gang warfare and new tensions brought by contingents of inmates from the newly acquired territories on the USSR's western borderlands. Far from stabilizing, then, the Gulag of the postwar era continued to be defined by chaos and contradiction.

The Wartime Gulag

For the Soviet Union, the Second World War started as a geopolitical triumph. The Nazi-Soviet Pact of 1939 allowed Stalin to forcibly annex part of Finland, the three Baltic states, a large chunk of Poland, part of Czechoslovakia, and Moldova. Most of these territories were formerly ruled by the Russian Empire but broke free shortly after the 1917 revolution. From 1939 to 1941, Stalin worked toward making these regions Soviet by establishing various political and Party organizations, holding unfree elections, engaging in pro-Soviet propaganda, and nationalizing economic property. He also unleashed class warfare and a search for various potential enemies. Hundreds of thousands of wealthy capitalists, members of the old military and police forces, religious authorities, and others suspected of opposing Soviet rule were sentenced to the Gulag or forcibly relocated to the special settlements of Central Asia.

A second wave of repression that increased the size of the Gulag stemmed from new labor laws that in 1940–41 resulted in the imprisonment of hundreds of thousands of Soviet subjects for absenteeism, laziness on the jobsite, or persistent tardiness. The purpose was to discipline Soviet society in preparation for the anticipated war with Germany. On the eve of war, therefore, the Gulag was expanding rapidly. Between 1939 and 1941, the inmate population in the USSR's prisons, corrective-labor colonies, and corrective-labor camps increased from 1.9 to 2.9 million. Most convicted for labor law violations only spent a few months in prison or a corrective-labor colony, but the camp population rose by some 250,000 people, many of them from the new Western borderlands. Such was the state of the Gulag when the war began.

In June 1941, Nazi Germany invaded the Soviet Union. The Red Army was quickly overwhelmed and German forces reached the outskirts of Moscow and Leningrad within months. There, Soviet defenses finally held, and the following years featured a brutal war that was ultimately won by the USSR in 1945. Socialism, it seemed, had triumphed over fascism. But victory in the Great Patriotic War, as the Soviets termed it, came at a steep price. Heavy combat fighting and the multiyear occupation of broad swaths of Soviet territory resulted in unfathomable destruction and the deaths of over 20 million Soviet subjects. Meanwhile, immense suffering defined Soviet life during the war years, and this was especially true for Gulag prisoners.

As Soviet forces retreated during the initial German advance, the Gulag scrambled to evacuate important personnel and resources eastward. This was made difficult by a shortage of railway cars, and many inmates recalled performing some of the evacuation on foot. The rapidity of the retreat ultimately meant that some of the 750,000 prisoners in the evacuation zone fell into German hands. In part to alleviate this pressure, Stalin decreed a mass release of short-term inmates, juveniles, invalids, pregnant mothers, and others deemed unfit for evacuation. Initially applied to just the western regions of the USSR, it soon resulted in the release of over 500,000 inmates across the entire Gulag system. Plus, as soon as the invasion began, many able-bodied Gulag prisoners petitioned to join the military to defend the Fatherland. More than 1,000,000 of them would have this wish granted, and over 60,000 special settlers and their families were also released. It may seem odd that Stalin would grant early release to over 1.5 million inmates who had been purposefully isolated from Soviet society. But the dire situation brought about by German invasion immediately changed the calculus of repression. Soldiers and military support personnel were desperately needed, and both prisoners and guards were sent to serve in these capacities. Thus, even those not released to join the army (the old, sick, and pregnant) helped free up valuable manpower by reducing the need for Gulag guards.

Most political prisoners, however, were not released, despite patriotic pleas made in a bid to join the Red Army. Stalin decided they were not trustworthy and kept them in the Gulag as forced laborers instead. Indeed, it became common during the war for Gulag officials to refer to these "enemies of the people" as fascists, putting them directly on par with the German soldiers killing Soviet citizens. Common criminals in the Gulag mimicked this language and increased their own verbal and physical abuse of political prisoners without fear of retribution. Moreover, tens of thousands of political prisoners were sent to special *katorga* camps that took their name from the tsarist system of hard labor in Siberian exile. These camps, according to Solzhenitsyn, blended "all that was worst in the camps with all that was worst in the prisons."[1] Inmates were subjected to strict discipline, heavy surveillance, increased labor hours, and often more dangerous work assignments. And although the head of the Gulag asserted that even such camps were fundamentally correctional in nature, this was an abject lie. Rather, the *katorga* camps quickly became the site of sickness, exhaustion, and premature death.

But even for the majority of inmates who remained in the regular camps and colonies of the Gulag, life and labor became more difficult as Stalin quickly moved the penal system, like the rest of the Soviet economy, to a wartime footing. Hours were increased to twelve or more per day and days off became less frequent. This mirrored but also exceeded similar changes to labor expectations outside of the Gulag, where Soviet citizens were pushed to work eleven hour shifts and exceed their labor norms. For some inmates, as in broader Soviet society, the nature of their work changed to prioritize items needed for the war effort. Gulag prisoners began producing uniforms, artillery shells, rifles, and other wartime necessities; some 10 to 15 percent of all ammunition manufactured during the war years was made using inmate labor.[2] They also constructed airfields and built antitank defenses. And the pressure on Gulag bosses to reach production targets was intense. As one remembered being instructed concerning an urgent task, "If you pull this off, you will get an award; if you don't, we will shoot you."[3]

Gulag officials were quick to trumpet their contribution to the war effort in their monthly and yearly reports to Moscow. The importance of production also featured heavily in increasing numbers of patriotic speeches delivered by Gulag officials. Inmates were constantly reminded of the extreme importance of their labor: without the coal they were mining or the food they were harvesting or the ammunition they were producing, the war over fascism could not be won. As one Gulag administrator instructed his subordinates who were delivering such messages, they were to "call forth a feeling of hatred for the bloody and vile enemy" and convince the inmates to "work not just for yourself but for your comrade who has gone to the front."[4] Such messages no doubt had a patriotic effect on some prisoners who felt indignant at the German invasion against their homeland. But others rejected such calls to redouble their efforts and continued working as little as possible in the interest of their own personal survival.

Indeed, survival was no easy task during the war years. For most Gulag inmates, the war meant not just increased labor demands but increasingly insufficient food. With the most important grain-producing regions—Ukraine, Belarus, and southwestern Russia—in German hands, Soviet subjects experienced widespread hunger during the war years. If high-ranking officials and soldiers were the highest priority in terms of food distribution, prisoners were deemed the lowest. Starvation conditions in the camps swiftly developed, as remembered by Lev Razgon: "Within two to three months the camp was full of living skeletons …. Carts and then sledges carried the almost weightless bodies to the cemetery each morning."[5] According to official statistics, 1942 and 1943 were the deadliest years of Gulag operations, with mortality rates exceeding by 20 percent. For the four years of war taken together, the Gulag recorded over 800,000 deaths, but these figures were certainly undercounts of those who actually died in the Gulag or shortly after release. Gulag officials could get in trouble if too many of their inmates died, so one widespread practice was to grant early release to those about to die. Taking this into account it is certain that well over a million Gulag inmates died during the war.[6]

A final important development that affected both the Gulag and the special settlements was the mass arrests and deportations of several national minority groups. These started during the Soviet annexations of 1939–40, but Stalin then launched a second round of deportations in 1943–44, meting out revenge against those suspected of disloyalty against the USSR during German occupation. The Chechen, Ingush, Crimean Tatar, Balkar, and Kalmyk peoples were most prominent among these, with over a million men, women, and children summarily deported to Central Asia or Siberia. Almost 1 million Volga Germans, whose ancestors had lived in Russia for centuries, were also deported during the war due to suspicion of mixed loyalties, a motive similar to the internment of Japanese Americans by the United States at the same time. Thus, by the end of the war, the special settlements were no longer dominated by *kulaks* and their families from the collectivization drive of the early 1930s. Non-Russian minority groups were now the primary occupants.

Like Gulag inmates, special settlers were compelled to labor for the war effort. They could not leave their assigned place of exile, and the secret police created a network of informants among them to help monitor their actions and attitudes. In some locations they lived next to a Gulag camp and labored with the inmates. But their status as settlers rather than inmates meant they had some localized freedom of movement that at times raised suspicions among the local populations. As one Soviet official in Western Siberia, worried about ethnically German settlers, expressed, "at times this roaming around by fascist elements is used to establish connections with counter-revolutionary goals."[7] Some settlers were, in fact, executed for alleged treason or else sent to the Gulag for various other offenses. Of course, many relocated settlers had anti-Soviet attitudes—they had been forcibly removed from their homes on the flimsiest of pretexts, which no doubt produced hatred toward the Soviet regime. But that did not mean they were collaborating with the enemy or actively conspiring to overthrow the USSR.

Most exiles were not executed or sentenced to the Gulag, but they still suffered immensely during the war. Their forced deportation meant a painful relocation from their homeland and separation from family and friends, all while enduring harsh working conditions and food scarcity.[8] As one settler recalled, they "were forced to work on the [collective farm] from dawn to dusk, and weren't given even a single gram of bread, a single penny in wages ... Then the starvation began; people withered away to skeletons, and began to fall."[9] Another, remembering the squalid living conditions, terrible rations, and hard labor, affirmed that "nothing differentiated us from our 'colleagues' from the neighboring camp."[10] Malaria in the cotton-growing regions of Central Asia was widespread and deadly, killing tens of thousands of settlers. Others suffered serious respiratory diseases and eye ailments from the cotton pollen and dust. In all, around 20 percent of all German exiles and a similar percent of other nationalities died during or shortly after the war, comprising around 450,000 deaths.

The high death toll of the targeted ethnic deportations of the 1930s and 1940s has prompted some scholars to label them genocides. Genocide, a term that was coined to make sense of the Holocaust, has been defined variously, but the most commonly accepted definition comes from the United Nations' 1948 Convention on the Prevention and Punishment of the Crime of Genocide. The Convention defines genocide as "acts committed with the intent to destroy, in whole or in part, a national, ethnic, racial or religious group." This can include not only mass killing, but also other actions, including "deliberately inflicting on the group conditions of life calculated to bring about its physical destruction."[11] The ethnic deportations ordered by Stalin for the most part did not feature widespread killing, but arguably did fit the "conditions of life" clause. Whether Stalin intended for such widespread death to occur among deportees is a more difficult question—there are no documents attesting to such an intent. Yet the overall body of evidence has prompted some historians to conclude that the deportations, if not a clear cut case of genocide, met some of the criteria.[12] Certainly, if not genocide, the deportations fall under the broader category of "crimes against humanity," defined at the post-Second World War Nuremberg Trials as "murder, extermination, enslavement, deportation, and other inhumane acts committed against any civilian population ... or persecutions on political, racial or religious grounds."[13] Indeed, many actions taken by the Soviet Union, especially under Stalin, fit squarely within this definition.

Exporting the Gulag

The Second World War was a traumatic yet transformational event for the Soviet Union. It brought death and destruction but also a sense of righteous accomplishment in defeating the Nazi menace. To Stalin, victory seemed to justify Soviet-style socialism, and some people in neighboring countries shared this view. After the war, indigenous communist movements, combined with heavy-handed Soviet military occupation, led Poland, East Germany, Czechoslovakia, Hungary, Romania, Bulgaria, Yugoslavia, Albania, China, and North Korea to adopt Marxist ideology and political dictatorship. Soviet "advisers" helped establish government, military, police, economic, social, and educational institutions in these countries, and worked to bind them to the USSR. Among these Soviet advisers were legal experts and penal officials who wrote new legal codes and set up penal systems modeled on the Gulag.

The most infamous of these copycat penal systems was the *laogai* (literally "reform through labor") of the People's Republic of China. Similar to its Soviet counterpart, it featured hundreds of camps and prisons that held not only ordinary criminals but also political and religious ones as well. Inmates, many convicted through sham legal processes, underwent intensive re-educational programming along with hard labor in an effort to turn them into loyal, submissive citizens. And like the Gulag, this was a brutal system marked by high mortality rates caused by starvation, exhaustion, and physical violence. Officials declared that inmates "had a duty to produce 'material riches' in exchange for forgiveness from the collective."[14] And the result, as described by former inmate Harry Wu, was hard labor, insufficient rations, and violence and humiliation from the guards. Of a particularly brutal year marked by famine he recalled, "I don't know how many sick prisoners died that October. I don't even know how many died in my squad .... Dead bodies went out and live bodies came in almost daily. I paid no attention. I never even learned their names."[15]

The Soviet satellite states of Eastern Europe pursued similar systems of detention, some for convicted prisoners and others for suspected ideological opponents. Special camps under jurisdiction of the Soviet Gulag opened in East Germany, a few of them on the territory of former German concentration camps. These were "organized and laid out according to Soviet design in the same way as the GULAG camps in the Soviet Union with minimal rations, poor medical services, and overcrowded barracks."[16] Tens of thousands of people—former Nazis, political opponents, class enemies, and common criminals—died in these camps from 1945 to 1950. Yugoslavia set up penal camps on the uninhabited islands of Goli Otok and Sveti Grgur and sent a variety of people to labor and suffer there. In Bulgaria, the Belene "labor-educational commune," located on an island in the Danube River, held thousands of political and religious prisoners who had not been convicted of a crime. Forced labor camps dotted the Hungarian countryside, where "enemies of the people" were beaten, humiliated, and forced to labor for long hours in primitive living conditions. As István Fehérváry remembered, the inmates quickly "became weak and skeletal, resembling the victims of the concentration camps."[17] Similar institutions were set up in Poland, Czechoslovakia, Romania, and Albania.

Some people in these countries, however, were arrested and sent to the Soviet Gulag itself. Thousands of Slovaks, for instance, were deported to labor camps in the USSR for their perceived loyalty to the Nazis. Many never returned and those who did "were branded as enemies of socialism."[18] Michael Solomon similarly wrote of his own experience of being seized in his native Romania in 1948, sentenced to "25 years labor in the penal working camps of the Siberian extreme north," and transferred to the Gulag camps of Kolyma.[19] The Gulag after the Second World War thus not only served as the penal system for Soviet citizens, but also held over 10,000 foreigners from East Bloc countries.

The Postwar Gulag

The Soviet Union celebrated victory in the Second World War with victory parades, speeches, medals, and even a mass amnesty of Gulag prisoners. The Soviet Union routinely employed amnesties to commemorate anniversaries of the Bolshevik Revolution and other important dates, but the amnesty of 1945 was unusually large in scope: some 620,000 inmates were released and another 212,000 had their sentences halved. As was typical of Soviet amnesties, political prisoners and those with multiple convictions were excluded, a fact deeply resented by those who felt themselves wrongly convicted in the first place. As Solzhenitsyn, who had only recently been arrested for criticizing Stalin's wartime leadership in letters to friends, bitterly expressed, this was an amnesty "for deserters, swindlers, and thieves."[20]

The reduced Gulag population did not last for long, however. As the deputy commander of the Gulag presciently remarked at the time of the amnesty, "the loss of freed prisoners will be offset by the influx of new prisoners into camps and colonies."[21] This repopulation happened due to the regular course of Soviet policing, but multiple waves of repression also made this prophecy come true. First, large numbers of Soviet subjects from the western regions of the USSR were sentenced to years in the Gulag "for active counter-revolutionary activity in the period of the German-Fascist occupation."[22] The same fate befell many Red Army soldiers who had been captured by German forces and held in POW camps. Their survival implied that they had betrayed the USSR in some way, the thinking went, not least by surrendering rather than fighting to the death. Soviet camps and exile settlements were also filled by another round of class warfare and Sovietization in the newly acquired territories on its western borderland. As in 1939–41, hundreds of thousands of Estonians, Latvians, Lithuanians, Poles, Belarusians, Ukrainians, and Moldovans were sent to the Gulag or the special settlements after the war's conclusion.

A final act of repression in the immediate postwar context came in 1947 when the Soviet Union issued new anti-theft laws. Passed amidst famine conditions, the laws punished even minor acts of theft or embezzlement with long sentences. By the end of 1950, over 1 million prisoners in the Gulag had been convicted by these laws, representing around 40 percent of all inmates. Combined, these postwar repressive measures raised the Gulag population to its highest levels ever. By the early 1950s, some 2.5 million people were imprisoned in the camps and colonies of the Gulag, along with hundreds of thousands in prison. Another 2.5 million were detained in the special settlements.

As for political prisoners, two significant developments occurred in the postwar period. First, rather than release many "counterrevolutionaries" who had been sentenced to ten-year terms in

1937–38, Stalin had them retried and left in the Gulag or else sentenced to exile upon their release from the camps. Eugenia Ginzburg, as a representative example, was released in 1947 but was given a six-year exile term and prevented from leaving the Kolyma region. In 1949, she was arrested again and given permanent exile status. At this Ginzburg expressed relief, "for exile is not camp. There's no guard, no barbed wire, one is allowed to live in one's own hovel, with one's own nearest and dearest around one."[23] Stalin thus ensured that those arrested during the Great Terror were kept isolated and under the watch of the secret police.

The other reform that affected political prisoners was the 1948 creation of "special camps" designed to hold "spies, saboteurs, terrorists, Trotskyites, rightists, Mensheviks, SRs, anarchists, nationalists, white emigrants and participants in other anti-Soviet organizations and groups and those presenting danger by their anti-Soviet ties and enemy activities."[24] Notable is the continued use of political categories that dated back to the civil war era, showing how much the Soviet worldview was shaped by those pivotal early years. The effect of this decree was to separate hundreds of thousands of political prisoners from common criminals. These special camps featured an intentionally punishing penal regimen that closely resembled the *katorga* camps (which still existed, holding nearly 30,000 inmates in 1950). Inmates endured fewer privileges, harsher living conditions, increased surveillance, and bars and locks on the barracks to prevent social mixing after work. Perhaps most significant for the inmates were the numbers on their uniforms by which they were addressed by camp officials. As Janusz Bardach related, "You were nameless: just a numbered object to be thrown in the cooler if you failed to conform and thrown in the death wagon with your number wired to your big toe if you failed to survive."[25] This small but significant act signified their descent into nameless, dehumanized repression.

As the size of the Gulag expanded, so did its economic profile. Michael Solomon recalled his camp commander informing new arrivals that "We need metal, and you must produce this metal according to The Plan. The fulfillment of The Plan is our sacred duty. Those who do not fulfill The Plan are saboteurs and traitors, and we show them no mercy."[26] Ultimately, many of the large construction projects that inmates labored on in the late Stalin era would, like the White Sea—Baltic Sea Canal of the early 1930s, cost a fortune in resources and human lives while providing little economic benefit to the country. The Salakhard-Igarka Railway, later dubbed the "road of death" or "railroad to nowhere," epitomized these projects. Planned to transverse over 800 miles of the Siberian arctic, it ultimately was abandoned with only a few hundred miles completed.[27]

In order to spur productivity, the Gulag re-introduced incentive programs that had earlier been abolished. The first was a system of wages paid to prisoners who fulfilled or overfulfilled their labor norms. These were not large, just a fraction of the wages of free workers, and theft and a vastly increased scale of bribery quickly became a problem. As historian Alan Barenberg has found, the new wages meant that illicit "cash payments accompanied many transactions within the camp and were essential in order to secure favors or services from fellow prisoners who held superior positions in the camp hierarchy."[28] But the cash infusions did allow inmates to purchase additional food at camp stores or new cash-only cafeterias that opened in the early 1950s as more food became available in the country at large. The second reform was the restoration of the workday credit system that had been abolished in 1939. Many inmates, though not those in the special camps, were thereby able to reduce their sentences through hard work and good behavior.

Changes to Inmate Society

As a result of the war and its associated episodes of repression, the last several years of Stalin's reign witnessed two new changes to the lived experience of the Gulag: a large contingent of inmates from the western borderlands and the rise of powerful criminal gangs. First, although the Gulag prior to 1939 was somewhat multiethnic, the sudden influx of hundreds of thousands of inmates from Estonia, Latvia, Lithuania, western Belarus, western Ukraine, and Moldova changed the dynamics of inmate society. These inmates brought with them their own languages and cultures and they tended to stick together in the camps, self-sorting by nationality. Relations among the various ethnic groups were often but not always harmonious; as Michael Solomon related of his own experience, mutual suspicion among Russians, Ukrainians, Jews, and Germans "could easily turn to malice and even murder."[29] But within ethnic groups a strong sense of solidarity and mutual support often developed. As another inmate recalled, "All the Ukrainians stuck together, as this gave us strength. We remembered our traditions and felt ourselves a tiny part of our homeland."[30]

An important part of these traditions for many newly arrived inmates was religion. As Nina Gagen-Torn recalled of this infusion of religiosity, "The range of religious beliefs was astonishing …. The Russian Orthodox gather under one tree. Under another stand the 'westerners,' the Uniates. Then there are the Baptists …. Two Catholics find their own corner, and under the scornful gaze of the rest of the worshippers, begin praying in Latin."[31] Sometimes religious arguments would break out, but more often there was a shared sense of mutual respect. Aleksandr Solzhenitsyn made rosaries in the camp with a group of Lithuanian Catholics and admired their "true brotherly love."[32] John Noble recalled that Lutherans from Estonia and Latvia began meeting to pray, study the Bible, sing hymns, and listen to sermons. Baptists from Ukraine then started preaching covertly, trying to convert other inmates to their faith. Yet, as Noble observed, "differences in denominations or creed were much less important in Vorkuta than in the outside world. We were all standing together against the common foe."[33] This sense of opposition to Soviet power by prisoners from the western borderlands, whether out of religious or nationalist motivations, was often noted by Gulag inmates and guards. Iryna Mateshuk-Hrytsyna recalled that "women from different nations were drawn to us Ukrainians, but especially girls from the Baltics—the Lithuanians, Estonians, and Latvians—who considered themselves very close in spirit, in the struggle for the freedom of their people."[34]

The second important development in Gulag society after the war was the rise of powerful criminal gangs. Gangs certainly existed in the prisons and camps of the 1920s and 1930s, but they were typically local in nature, focused on thieving, gambling, and humiliating other inmates as they banded together for protection and comradery. As Janusz Bardach related of getting on the wrong side of a local gang in a Kolyma camp, "they stole my bread, beat me, spat on me. More than the physical pain, it was the cruelty and hatred that drove me to despair."[35] For those in the gangs this was, in the words of historian Mark Vincent, "intended to aid their own solidarity and chances of survival."[36] During and especially after the Second World War, gangs became larger and more influential in inmate society. Some of these were national gangs comprised of inmates from the western borderlands, from Transcaucasia, or from Central Asia, who banded together for self-protection. Indeed, as historian Mark Galeotti notes, the "constant mingling of criminals from across the Soviet Union" facilitated gang activity, with "the camp system ... at once enforcing and teaching underworld orthodoxy."[37]

By far the most important gang in the Gulag was the "thieves-in-law," or "honest thieves." They were so named after their "prisoner code," which instructed them to support each other, live only off illicit activities, and refuse to work for or otherwise cooperate with Soviet authorities. Some thieves did work, but only in select capacities—typically those that allowed them to pilfer supplies or acquire weapons or alcohol. The thieves-in-law operated as a loose network in all major camps and were often powerful enough to dictate certain aspects of camp operations, such as labor assignments. That many of them could get away with not working in institutions designed around mandatory labor illustrates the power they held over fellow inmates and guards alike, who were typically forced to provide cover for the thieves on threat of violence. And with that power the thieves-in-law "terrorized and abused [other prisoners], stealing their food and clothing, forcing them from the warmer bunks in the barracks, beating, even raping, with virtual impunity."[38] Memoirs from the postwar Gulag are replete with such accounts. Michael Solomon, for instance, recalled that "innocent people were savagely beheaded with axes in broad daylight or stabbed to death with picks and shovels. And always, no other prisoner or guard dared intervene to save the victim."[39]

In many camps in the postwar Gulag, however, the thieves-in-law were opposed by rival gangs of former thieves and others who actively collaborated with camp authorities for their own benefit. The thieves (and many others who mimicked the thieves' language) pejoratively called them "bitches," and conflict between them came to be known collectively in the postwar era as the "bitches' war." Camp authorities were at times complicit in stoking this gang violence by siding with either the thieves or their adversaries; one tactic was to place a few of one group in a camp zone dominated by the other group. As inmate Anatoly Zhigulin explained, "thieves finding themselves in a bitches' [camp] ... would often find themselves facing a dilemma: die, or become a bitch. Likewise, if a large group of thieves arrived at a [camp] all of the bitches would hide ... when the regime changed, there were often bloody results."[40] At other times, though, camp authorities attempted to keep the gangs apart in order to keep the violence from preventing fulfillment of the camp's production targets.

Conclusions

The Soviet Gulag in the 1940s and early 1950s expanded, then contracted, then expanded again, with an array of political, ethnic, and criminal inmates arriving in successive waves of repression. Taken together with the tumultuous 1930s, approximately 18–20 million people spent time in the Stalinist Gulag, in addition to millions more who were sent to special settlements and other forms of exile. These are truly staggering numbers in a country of between 150 and 190 million people. And while many of them served their sentence and were released, millions perished. According to the Gulag's own records, some 1.6 million Gulag prisoners died during their period of incarceration. But historians have identified some whose deaths were not included in this count, including those who died in transit after sentencing. Moreover, as noted above, this official number fails to capture those who died shortly after their release, and it was common practice for Gulag bosses to release inmates on the verge of death in order to evade accountability. How many additional deaths should be added to the official tally is difficult to establish. Historians have studied this issue extensively and have proposed between

850,000 and 4 million additional deaths that can be attributed to the Gulag. In total, then, between 2.5 and 6 million people died during or shortly after their period of incarceration.

To revisit questions raised above in relation to the ethnic deportations, the Gulag for me clearly fits the definition of a crime against humanity. It was the mass imprisonment of tens of millions of civilians, many innocent of any crime—even by the USSR's own legal code—or given long periods of incarceration for relatively minor crimes. Moreover, this was a system that featured several of the other criteria for a crime against humanity as defined by the Rome Statute (1998) of the International Criminal Court: torture, sexual violence, coerced labor, and "other inhumane acts of a similar character intentionally causing great suffering."[41] Thousands of memoirs, official documents, and other sources attest to such conditions.

The case for genocide, however, is far from clear. First, the Gulag itself did not target a specific group of people. Men, women, young people, old people, Russians, Ukrainians, Kazakhs, Estonians, Chechens, atheists, Christians, Muslims, Jews, Communists, capitalists, peasants, shopkeepers, engineers, professors, soldiers, and politicians all suffered in the Gulag. Second, the question of intent to exterminate inmates is also difficult to pin down in relation to the Gulag, despite the high death toll. Stalin was certainly willing to employ execution, but once people were sentenced to the Gulag they were supposed to be kept alive (as long as they worked and behaved properly). That Gulag officials could get in trouble for too many inmates dying speaks against the question of intentional extermination. And yet, year after year the Gulag failed to create conditions that would reasonably *prevent* the millions of deaths that occurred. And some historians see in that enough evidence to make a case for the intention to exterminate. But even if we consider that the Gulag itself lacked murderous intent against a specific group for it to qualify for genocide (even while other crimes of the Stalin era may have risen to this standard), this in no way lessens the magnitude of this crime against humanity. Millions died unjustly and millions more suffered terribly both during and after their period of incarceration.

CHAPTER 5
THE GULAG AFTER STALIN

By the time of Stalin's death in 1953, the Gulag was enormous and economically important for the Soviet state, but it was also laden with problems. Low productivity and the persistent waste of both manpower and materials plagued the Gulag system and, in fact, a proposal drafted by the secret police in 1951 looked into converting about 70 percent of Gulag inmates into exiles. This would reduce state expenditures and in theory boost productivity, but Stalin rejected this plan and the Gulag remained intact. There was also growing concern at Gulag headquarters about violence among prisoners and increasing defiance of camp authorities by both gangs and inmates from the western borderlands. In response, the Gulag increased the number of guards from 91,000 in 1947 to 223,000 in 1951, a much faster proportional increase than the growth of the inmate population. But unrest among the inmates continued unabated. These issues of economic waste and defiant prisoners have led some historians to argue that the system was reaching a breaking point.[1] Other historians have argued that these very real problems were ultimately manageable, and that it was only Stalin's death and ensuing reforms that made the late-Stalin Gulag appear in hindsight to be on the verge of collapse.[2]

In either case, Joseph Stalin died on March 5, 1953, after nearly thirty years in power. His death and the ensuing power struggle among his top lieutenants raised many questions about which aspects of the Soviet system might be transformed or abolished. Ultimately, Nikita Khrushchev seized power and initiated reforms designed to make Soviet-style socialism more dynamic and less repressive. He denounced Stalin as a murderous dictator, relaxed censorship, increased spending on consumer goods, promoted international cultural and educational exchanges, and encouraged "peaceful coexistence" with the West.

Many of these campaigns, however, were only partially effective due to Khrushchev's own shortcomings as a leader and the Stalinist legacy that still pervaded the Soviet system. Perhaps nothing illustrates this better than his attempted transformation of the Gulag; although Khrushchev dramatically reduced the size of the Gulag, he was only partly successful in reorienting its internal mission and operations. In the end, the Gulag endured.

In 1964, Khrushchev was sacked in a bloodless coup and replaced by Leonid Brezhnev, who ruled into the early 1980s. Brezhnev emphasized stability rather than reform, and many aspects of Soviet life and governance, including the Soviet penal system, stagnated. Few reforms or innovations were introduced from the late 1960s to the mid-1980s, and the number of Gulag prisoners grew slowly in proportion to growth in the national population. Tension between the central goals of isolation, re-education, retribution, and cost control persisted, but Gulag administrators exhibited little enthusiasm for any of these aims. And while not as abusive or deadly as Stalin's Gulag, Brezhnev's Gulag was still a place of suffering caused by corrupt guards and chronic underfunding. Reforms initiated in the late 1980s by the last Soviet leader, Mikhail Gorbachev, brought a few important changes to the Gulag, but Gorbachev's broader reforms ultimately resulted in the collapse of the Soviet economy and then the Soviet Union itself in December 1991.

The Khrushchev Era

Stalin's death was the most significant event for the Soviet Union since the victory over Nazi Germany in 1945. It was at once destabilizing—Stalin had been in power since the 1920s and did not choose an heir prior to his passing—and cause for cautious optimism. Nowhere were these dual emotions more prevalent than in the Gulag. Guards and administrators became hesitant in their actions, unsure as to how Stalin's death would affect camp operations. Inmates expressed a range of emotions, from distress and sadness to intense jubilation. Regardless of their feelings toward Stalin, many inmates hoped for release or at least improved conditions. As Eugenia Ginzburg, then in exile after more than ten years of imprisonment, expressed, "Everyone's head was spinning with the expectation of imminent change."[3]

Indeed, change came quickly. For some historians, impressed by the magnitude of reform, the Gulag ceased to exist shortly after Stalin's death. According to this interpretation, the massive system of forced labor built in the 1930s to house opponents of the regime was a central feature of Stalinism. With Stalin dead, that system was then "dismantled" by his successors in the mid-1950s.[4] Other scholars insist that the Gulag as a place of political repression and slave labor was fundamental not to Stalinism but to the Soviet system itself. In this conception, the Gulag long outlasted Stalin. As Aleksandr Solzhenitsyn succinctly declared, "Rulers change, the Archipelago remains."[5] More recently, a third group of historians have forged a middle ground, arguing that the Gulag as a hybrid penal-camp system was not abolished but was fundamentally changed. In this view, the Gulag persisted but abandoned "unchecked (and even abetted) violence, grueling labor, and oppressive living conditions—the defining features of the Stalinist penal system."[6] Never again would it be a place of intense suffering, torture and mass death, nor would it hold hundreds of thousands of innocent people.

With those interpretations in mind, we will now turn to the motivations and then the details of the post-Stalin Gulag reforms. The logic behind the post-Stalin reform movement is complicated and somewhat unclear. Both Lavrenty Beria, who initiated a series of sweeping Gulag reforms immediately after Stalin's death, and Nikita Khrushchev, who deepened this drive after Beria was arrested and executed, used reforms as a way to advance their own political power during the post-Stalin power struggle. For Beria, who was intimately familiar with the Gulag, the rationalization was primarily economic. He well understood the economic inefficiency of the Gulag and looked to downsize and reform the system to boost economic productivity both in and outside of the camps. For Khrushchev, there seems to have been genuine regret regarding his own role in Stalinist repression and a desire to atone for the past. He recognized the brutality of the labor camp system and in 1956 famously condemned Stalin's repression of innocent people in his not-so-secret "Secret Speech."

But there were also developments in the Gulag that may have spurred the post-Stalin reforms. In 1953 and 1954, three major uprisings in special camps near Vorkuta, Norilsk, and Karaganda, along with numerous smaller revolts in regular camps, shook the Gulag system. Tens of thousands of inmates—mostly political prisoners and inmates from the western borderlands—protested against guard brutality, poor living conditions, curtailed rights, and the imprisonment of people who had committed no crime. The strikers refused to work, expelled guards from the living zones of the camps, and asked for judicial reviews of their cases along with better living conditions. Some demanded immediate release and threatened violence. Others sought negotiation while striking a patriotic tone, such as by displaying banners that read "Long live the Soviet regime!"[7]

In each of the three major uprisings, Gulag authorities from Moscow negotiated directly before ultimately putting the strikes down through military force. Though unsuccessful in that sense, the uprisings certainly caused the country's top leadership, who received regular reports of the proceedings, to question the purpose and operational regimen of the country's penal system. Substantive Gulag reforms began before the first of these uprisings, but the uprisings may have helped to deepen the reforming drive, particularly in relation to political prisoners. The special camps, for instance, were abolished soon after the uprisings, seemingly in direct response to the strikers' demands.[8] But motivations among the country's leadership were complex and force historians to make assumptions in the absence of introspective primary source documents detailing their thoughts at the time.

Whether prompted by economic or humanitarian concerns or compelled by inmate uprisings, the post-Stalin reforms were significant. Crucially, the Gulag underwent a significant reduction in size. Mass amnesties, the expanded use of parole and workday credits, the repatriation of incarcerated foreigners, and two rounds of judicial case reviews resulted in millions of people being released before the end of their sentences. This reduced the incarcerated population from some 2.5 million in 1953 to around 600,000 in 1960; over the same period the number of inmates sentenced for political crimes decreased even more significantly, from over 500,000 (around 20 percent of the total) to under 10,000 (less than 2 percent of the total). Moreover, the special settlements that held around 2.5 million people in 1953 were closed and most exiles were allowed to return home. The Soviet penal system by 1960 had not been so small since the 1920s, nor had there been so few political prisoners. It can be argued that the Gulag under Khrushchev was still an institution of mass incarceration—the USSR still had one of the highest rates of incarceration in the world—but it was mass incarceration on a much smaller scale than under Stalin.

Unfortunately for those released, the transition back into society was often difficult. Most continued to suffer physically or psychologically from the trauma of many years of harsh imprisonment. "It was clear that many of [the released] had no sense at all of how to manage on the outside," one prisoner recalled.[9] Many had lost friends and loved ones during their period of incarceration and had nowhere to go upon release. And although they had left the Gulag, former prisoners continued to be ostracized from the rest of society.[10] Moreover, many continued to be monitored by the secret police. As Ukrainian nationalist Danylo Shumuk related of a suspicious person who suddenly appeared at the state farm where he worked after release, "I was constantly aware of his persistent gaze, which followed me like a shadow ... and every day I became increasingly aware of the operation of this police machine."[11] Shumuk was soon arrested again and returned to the Gulag.

But some found ways to move past their Gulag experiences, at least to some extent. Many stayed near their camps in the remote corners of the Soviet Union—indeed, they were recruited to do so by local municipal authorities—which provided an easier transition regarding housing and employment.[12] Their labor was badly needed by economic managers, and other former prisoners provided a common set of experiences on which friendships could be built.[13] Perhaps more surprisingly, many repressed members of the Communist Party who were released from the Gulag after years of suffering maintained their beliefs in the Party and the Soviet system. This attitude helped them forge at least partially successful careers while viewing their period of unjust incarceration as an unfortunate detour in the country's transition to socialism.[14] As one committed communist related of her repressed father, "In jail they'd knocked his teeth out and crushed his skull. Still, my father didn't change his stripes, he remained a communist to the end of his life."[15]

Beyond the dramatic downsizing of the Gulag, Khrushchev and his allies pushed through reforms aimed at making the penal system more humane and re-educational. Stalin's camps, they concluded, were too large, violent, and production-centered, with the effect of making criminals worse rather than turning them into good Soviet citizens. As one Politburo member in 1954 remarked to his colleagues in a private meeting, the Gulag must "pay attention not to construction but to the correction of people."[16] As a result of this reorientation, numerous Gulag-staffed development projects were deemed wasteful and shuttered, resulting in a dramatically reduced economic portfolio. Renewed focus on re-education also produced an insistence that inmates of any background could be reformed. As Khrushchev proclaimed in 1959, speaking publicly of a former gangster with multiple convictions, "You need to believe in a man, in his good side. Can this man be an active participant in the construction of communism? He can, comrades!"[17]

To facilitate the re-education of criminals, Gulag guards and administrators were admonished to treat inmates not as enemies of the people but as wayward citizens who needed encouragement, understanding, and a measure of leniency. A more robust system of oversight over the Gulag weeded out noncompliant guards who continued to beat and humiliate the prisoners. Most of the large and remote camp complexes were replaced by smaller corrective-labor colonies with the purpose of keeping inmates in their home province for enhanced re-educational possibilities with family members and former co-workers. The working day was shortened and more resources were devoted to educational programs, vocational training, cultural programming, and athletic competitions [Figure 5.1]. Inmate self-governing bodies and procedures were instituted to give prisoners a voice in colony affairs and some buy-in for their own re-education.

Figure 5.1 Lithuanian political prisoners playing basketball in the Vorkutinsky Camp, mid-1950s.

Criminal gangs that terrorized their fellow inmates were largely broken up. Food rations increased and medical care improved, resulting in a healthier prisoner population. Efforts were also made to combat homosexual relations—viewed by Soviet authorities as corruptive to a healthy social order.[18]

Interestingly, these reforms were acknowledged in the Soviet press as Khrushchev, to some extent, lifted the veil of secrecy surrounding the Gulag. Academic journals actively discussed how the Gulag could be reformed and conferences of legal experts and Gulag administrators were convened to share ideas. The Khrushchev regime even invited a host of foreign observers to see how the Gulag had been turned into a model penal system that the West should emulate rather than criticize.[19] And former inmates recalled the tangible effect of these post-Stalin reforms. One wrote that "our daily menu suddenly became varied, an exciting alternative to the dull sameness," while another expressed pleasure that "by 1955 we had already stuffed ourselves with bread! And sheets even appeared."[20] Inmates enjoyed visits from family members, no longer had to shave their heads, and received more days free from labor. One found his camp, with spacious barracks, flower-lined paths, and billiards in the camp club, "just like a resort."[21] Likewise, the reduction of violence and the changed attitude among many guards was noticed. "It was as if something human had suddenly been awakened," one former inmate recalled.[22]

Yet ultimately these reforms were not entirely successful. An entrenched Gulag bureaucracy never fully embraced the new emphasis on re-education, overseers failed to catch all abuses perpetrated by guards, criminal gangs persisted to some extent, and recidivism continued. Perhaps most significantly, the Gulag never abandoned economic production either as a re-educational tool or as a way to recoup the costs of imprisonment, which led to persistent impulses to prioritize output over other goals. By 1960, a new wave of retributive attitudes among the Soviet citizenry and the country's top leadership resulted in a campaign to reduce "privileges" and tighten discipline in the Gulag. Things certainly did not return to the levels of violence, abuse, and privation seen in the Stalin-era Gulag, but this campaign halted and to some extent reversed efforts toward creating a more humane penal system. As Anatoly Marchenko explained of his time in the early 1960s, "the norm was such that you worked all day bent double and still could only just manage to fulfil it. And those who didn't and worked poorly had their parcels docked."[23]

As for political prisoners, the special camps were abolished in 1954, meaning the rapidly diminishing numbers of political prisoners were held alongside common criminals. But after only a few years Khrushchev decided to again separate them out to prevent them from infecting other inmates with their supposedly anti-Soviet ideas. Four camps were designated for political prisoners, with most eventually concentrated in the 1960s in the Dubravny Camp, some 300 miles southeast of Moscow. This was also the destination for imprisoned religious sectarians—Jehovah's Witnesses, Baptists, Adventists, and various dissenters from the Orthodox Church—who were held in their own camp zones to prevent them from converting other inmates to Christianity. As Helene Celmina recounted of her experience with the Jehovah's Witness there, "although I said that I had been christened and had my own faith, they explained that it was their duty to share theirs."[24] For proselytizing, holding prayer meetings, and conducting additional religious activities in the camps, they and other religious inmates were subjected to intense scrutiny and attempts from correctional authorities to disprove their faith.

One final area of post-Stalin reform concerned capital punishment. After a brief experiment with abolishing the death penalty in 1947, Stalin reinstated it in 1950 for acts of treason, espionage, and sabotage. It was then extended in 1951 to serious crimes committed in the camps by Gulag prisoners. After Stalin's death, Khrushchev and his peers moved to a general policy of increased leniency concerning lawbreakers, with sentences for many crimes being significantly reduced. But they kept capital punishment and in 1954 made premeditated murder a capital crime. The list of crimes eligible for execution expanded in 1958 to include aggravated rape, then again in 1961 and 1962 to include large-scale theft of state property, currency speculation, and bribery involving large sums. As a result, between 1,000 and 3,000 people per year were executed from the mid-1950s to the mid-1960s. This was far fewer than during the 1930s and 1940s, but still many more than the similarly sized United States, which executed fewer than 700 total from the mid-1950s to mid-1960s. Thus, even as the Khrushchev era made the Gulag smaller, more humane, and less focused on retribution, the ultimate retributive act of capital punishment not only persisted but was applied to more crimes than in the last few years of Stalin's reign.

The Brezhnev Era

In late 1964, Leonid Brezhnev seized power from Khrushchev, his former political patron. Promising stability as a countermeasure to Khrushchev's impulsiveness, Brezhnev only tinkered with economic and other reforms while trying to promote social harmony and stability. The military and secret police enjoyed his patronage and to some extent he rehabilitated Stalin's image. But there were no episodes of mass repression other than the famed Prague Spring of 1968, in which the Soviet military crushed a popular reform movement in its

East Bloc ally of Czechoslovakia. This meant that the size of the Soviet Gulag remained relatively stable.

At the beginning of Brezhnev's rule, the Gulag held about 750,000 inmates.[25] That figure climbed slowly for eighteen years until it reached around 1.2 million by the time of Brezhnev's death in 1982, keeping it the largest penal system in the world. The Gulag would have grown larger had it not been for a reform initiated in the last year of Khrushchev's reign and then expanded under Brezhnev that released well-behaved inmates to labor at particular jobsites after a percentage of their sentence had been served. This was supposedly designed as a re-educational tool aimed at gradually restoring to convicts their liberties, but it also helped to prevent inmate overcrowding; over 100,000 inmates per year were diverted out of penal facilities in the late 1960s and early 1970s.[26]

Memoirs paint a bleak but rarely deadly picture of the Brezhnev-era Gulag. Communal living, strict regulations, drab buildings, barbed-wire fences, undernourishment, and poor medical attention defined daily life. Inmates occasionally played sports, read books from the library, watched films, and endured half-hearted attempts at political indoctrination; as imprisoned dissident Andrei Amalrik related of these, "as a rule, nobody listened to the droning of the lecturer, as the propagandists themselves realized."[27] Some inmates collaborated with the guards and put on armbands distinguishing them as members of the "Section of Internal Order" in exchange for better treatment and the hope of early release. Professional criminals stole from, beat, and occasionally raped or murdered other prisoners, though gang violence and abuses never approached the levels of the late Stalin era. And the criminals of the Brezhnev era often treated political prisoners with respect; as Vladimir Bukovsky remarked of his time in various colonies and prisons, "the attitude of the crooks to us political had completely changed .... Our relations with them were those of good neighbors."[28]

One thing that did not change was compulsory labor, though it was not nearly as long or backbreaking as under Stalin. In stark contrast to earlier periods, Amalrik assessed, the Gulag of his day was not "founded on economic needs," but compelling inmates to work was still an "unconscious" impulse for the stagnating regime.[29] And inmates continued their various schemes for getting out of work, including by self-mutilation. Indeed, corruption and laziness were rampant among both inmates and their jailers, which led to little meaningful economic output. And as Bukovsky found, the black market thrived: "With the help of the guards, the free workers, the drivers of the trucks who come to collect the furniture [produced in the colony], you can buy anything you like: vodka, tea, drugs."[30] Though at times the colonies and prisons of the Brezhnev-era Gulag felt repressive, even totalitarian in nature, at other times they were still remarkably chaotic and arbitrary. Strict guidelines existed, but everyone—prisoners and guards alike—found ways to circumvent them.

Although the number of political prisoners remained relatively small under Brezhnev, they certainly continued to exist. Political dissidents such as Andrei Sinyavsky, Yuli Daniel, Alexander Ginzburg, and Yuri Orlov were isolated alongside religious prisoners and nationalists from Ukraine, Lithuanian, and other non-Russian regions of the USSR. They were held primarily in Vladimir Central Prison and a few corrective-labor colonies in Perm province: Perm-35, Perm-36, and Perm-37. One inmate of Perm-36, Sergei Kovalyov, described the humiliation inflicted on the prisoners by the guards. One in particular, he recalled, "would just take pleasure in telling you, say, that you were turning into a sheep."[31] Kovalyov also recalled how a long list of detailed regulations was designed "to guarantee the option of selective enforcement." Prisoners could then be punished for such mundane things as buttoning their shirt the wrong way, even if the actual reason for punishment was something else.[32] But as Vladimir Bukovsky remembered, the hyper-bureaucratic Soviet state was by that point somewhat responsive to accounts of mistreatment sent to various officials: "all you have to do is to know the law and the system under which complaints are examined."[33] Thus, the dissidents were well known for writing endless petitions to Soviet and international authorities, complaining about their treatment and their trials, sometimes with good effect. When this failed, hunger strikes were pursued, with forced feeding administered by Gulag medical authorities to keep striking inmates alive.

But some political, nationalist, and religious prisoners endured a different type of imprisonment as the Brezhnev regime confined them either during a lengthy criminal investigation or else as part of their sentence in psychiatric wards. As Anatoly Marchenko explained of the most famous of these institutions, "the Serbsky Institute can proclaim as mad almost anyone with even the slightest abnormality in his psychology, or even completely normal people—if that is what the KGB wants."[34] Inmates thus confined were routinely tortured and abused by hospital staff; as one inmate related, "the orderlies, often in a drunken condition, constantly beat the patients, sometimes savagely. Furthermore, they set the patients to fight one another and laid 'bets' on them."[35] Various tranquilizer and other drugs were regularly administrated, and these often led to physical disfiguration and the actual deterioration of the inmates' mental health. As one women related of her imprisoned husband after visiting him in the psychiatric hospital, "it was impossible to recognize him. His eyes were full of pain and misery, he spoke with difficulty, … his inner strength was exhausted."[36] Such, it seems, was the desired outcome.

Perhaps paradoxically, these most recent decades of the Soviet Gulag—the 1960s through the 1980s—are the least well understood in large part because Russian archival documents covering this period have not been declassified as they have for the 1920s to the 1950s. Some internal records are accessible in other post-Soviet republics such as Estonia and Ukraine, but historians have not yet tapped into these collections in a systematic way. Hopefully more research will be done over the coming years to help better understand the Gulag of the late Soviet era.

The Collapse of the Soviet Union

After the death of Brezhnev and his two geriatric successors (Yuri Andropov and Konstantin Chernenko), Mikhail Gorbachev came to power in 1985 as a young, rising star of the Communist Party. He promised to breathe life into the stagnating Soviet system, drawing inspiration from Khrushchev's de-Stalinization and from the Prague Spring movement of 1968. In particular after the nuclear meltdown at Chernobyl in 1986, Gorbachev proclaimed that socialism worked best in the absence of secrecy and repression. "Socialism with a human face," the catchphrase of Prague Spring, was possible, Gorbachev insisted. He duly relaxed censorship, reintroduced some elements of capitalism into the economy, and made the political system more democratic in a bid to revitalize Soviet socialism.

Criminal justice received less attention than the political, economic, and social spheres, but a few important reforms were made. A lawyer by training, Gorbachev called for a "law-based state" in which political leaders and the Communist Party itself would be strictly subject to the law.[37] Over the following years, increased access to lawyers for defendants was granted, many political and economic crimes were wiped off the books, and the number of crimes subject to capital punishment was trimmed. Judges were also instructed to use more lenient punishments rather than imprisonment for a variety of crimes.[38] Finally, Gorbachev set up the Public Commission for Humanitarian Questions and Human Rights (also known as the Burlatsky Commission after its lead investigator), which was tasked with ensuring legal compliance with the Helsinki Accords and other international and domestic laws.

As for the Gulag, the number of prisoners in 1985 continued to rise, fueled in part by Gorbachev's anti-alcohol campaign. Imprisonment then leveled off in 1986 before plummeting from around 1.5 million Gulag inmates to some 750,000 by 1990. This brought imprisonment down to the levels of the Khrushchev era but still left the Soviet Union just before its collapse with one of the highest rates of incarceration in the world. But beyond this reduction in size, Gorbachev's Gulag reforms were not particularly ambitious. Soviet prisoners continued to be held in a vast network of corrective-labor colonies and prisons administered by the Ministry of Internal Affairs, and labor remained their primary preoccupation. Few investments were made to modernize penal facilities or hire qualified correctional personnel. Prisoners complained of poor rations, beatings from guards, and insufficient protection from other inmates. Indeed, criminal gangs gained ground in the late 1980s and early 1990s, wresting *de facto* control of some facilities away from the guards.

In a few areas, however, there were meaningful reforms. Like his predecessors, Gorbachev initially denied that there were political prisoners in the Soviet Union before ultimately admitting that there were. Subsequent releases, pressed for by foreign countries and nongovernmental organizations, reduced their number to the lowest levels since 1917, and changes to the legal code made it much more difficult to convict Soviet citizens for political dissent. By mid-1989 there were only a few dozen prisoners left in penal colony Perm-35 [Figure 5.2]. They experienced a mundane existence marked by poor but sufficient food, mandatory labor, stays in the penalty isolator for disobedience, and a resentful relationship between inmates and guards. As one prisoner told a visiting French reporter, "these people try to strip us of our dignity, since without it we have no more strength."[39] By the time of the Soviet Union's collapse in 1991 there were virtually no political prisoners left.

Figure 5.2 The last political prisoners at Perm-35, 1989.

Another reform was the introduction of religious instruction as part of the re-educational program. Gorbachev put a halt to faith-based persecution in the Soviet Union and ultimately embraced religion as a possible way to revitalize socialist society. For Gulag prisoners this meant being allowed to read the Bible and Quran, wear crosses and other religious symbols, and discuss faith openly. Priests, pastors, and Christian youth groups were invited to talk with and minister to the inmates, and such discussions began to replace political lectures devoted to Marxist ideology. Communion, baptisms, and even church weddings were performed behind bars in the last few years of the Soviet Union's existence. And this was all publicly reported on in the national press. One widely read literary journal in 1989, for instance, described the visit by Metropolitan Filaret of Kyiv to a nearby prison colony where the local authorities "had come to the conclusion that the camp system ... had done very little to re-educate criminal offenders and that it was time for a new and more 'human' approach." The Metropolitan spoke to the prisoners, distributed Christian literature, and secured the promise that a room for confession would be set aside where inmates could meet in private with Orthodox priests.[40] This was all a dramatic reversal from seven decades of repressing religious expression in places of confinement.

The release of political prisoners and the return of religion to the Gulag and to Soviet society more broadly highlight the deep ideological crisis of the Gorbachev era that ultimately helped bring about the collapse of the Soviet Union. Most people no longer believed in Marxism, and younger generations in particular had become cynical about the ideology that justified the creation of the USSR in the first place. Uncensored accounts of the Gulag, the Great Terror, the famines, and other Soviet crimes began to be published in the Soviet press in the late 1980s and early 1990s, all of which aggravated public frustration with Communist Party rule. Ultimately, after a failed hardliner coup in August 1991, the Soviet Union disintegrated into fifteen sovereign countries.

Conclusions

The Soviet Gulag as a hybrid penal system, combining elements of the penitentiary, the concentration camp, and exile, long outlasted Stalin's death. For nearly four more decades the Soviet repressive apparatus convicted and imprisoned large numbers of Soviet citizens, some for their religious activity or ideological opposition to the regime. The central tensions of this system, revolving around economic production, self-sufficiency, rehabilitation, isolation, and retribution, were never fully resolved. Indeed, after an initial spate of reforms in the Khrushchev era, the late Soviet Gulag, in an increasingly stagnating ideological environment, became more of a warehouse for criminals rather than an economic powerhouse or social laboratory.

The human toll of the Soviet Gulag was truly staggering. Millions of people died and millions more were physically and psychologically traumatized. For Solzhenitsyn and other commentators, a secondary consequence of the Gulag was how former inmates and guards brought the corruption, lies, and violence of the Gulag back into the broader population, infecting it with a cancer that then metastasized in Soviet society. Criminal subculture that was heavily conditioned by Gulag experience blossomed in the late Soviet era.[41] And Soviet society as a whole became conditioned to passively accept violence, corruption, and the abrogation of constitutionally guaranteed liberties.[42] In other words, even after the worst years of the Gulag under Stalin were over, its destructive influence continued to warp Soviet society.

CHAPTER 6
REMEMBERING THE GULAG AND ITS VICTIMS

If the Gulag was the Soviet Union's penal system, it formally ceased to exist on December 25, 1991, when Mikhail Gorbachev announced the dissolution of the USSR. At that moment it split into fifteen pieces, with each post-Soviet republic suddenly in charge of the prisons and penal colonies located in its territory. The largest of these successor systems is in Russia. Officially called the Federal Service for the Discharge of Punishments, it holds close to a half million inmates as of this writing in 2022. The national incarceration rate for Russia is around 330 per 100,000 people—higher than most other countries but much lower than the US rate of around 700 per 100,000 people. It is also much lower than the Stalinist rate of incarceration but in line with that of the Khrushchev and Brezhnev era. Much of the Russian penal system's physical plant—the prisons and "corrective colonies"—remains from the Soviet era. Though stripped of its Marxist ideology, the Gulag as a hybrid prison-concentration camp system is largely intact.

And it is not just the physical plant that resembles the Soviet Gulag. Observers and prisoners alike decry the system's corruption, violence, poor treatment of inmates, continued insistence on inmate labor, and mere lip service to the idea of rehabilitation.[1] Observers of the post-Soviet penal system further highlight the imprisonment of Vladimir Putin's outspoken critics: businessman Mikhail Khodorkovsky, the members of the punk band Pussy Riot, and political opposition figure Alexey Navalny prominent among them. Thus, both the physical and practical complexities of the Gulag have endured in some form to the present day. As one prisoner's girlfriend in 2004 remarked of his conditions of imprisonment, "read Solzhenitsyn's *Gulag Archipelago*; it's just the same today—nothing has changed."[2]

This final chapter will examine not the Russian penal system, however, but the ways in which the Soviet Gulag has been both commemorated and forgotten from the Gorbachev era onward. That Russia has struggled with how to cope with the memory of the Gulag should not be surprising. Many countries grapple with the delicate issue of remembering atrocities perpetrated not by an external power but by a government against its own people. From Germany's long process of coming to terms with the Holocaust to the United States' refusal to build a national slavery museum, conscious downplaying, denial, and forgetting are common outcomes in similar contexts. Indeed, many scholars have accused the Russian government of deliberately ignoring the crimes of the Soviet era, of whitewashing the past in an effort to construct a positive, even triumphal vision of the Russian nation. And yet one finds across the Russian geographical and cultural landscape numerous instances of both "hard memory" (monuments and museums) and "soft memory" (art and literature) devoted to the Gulag.[3] These have been created by both state and non-state actors and take a variety of forms. But as much as they reveal a desire to not forget the imprisonment and death of millions of people, they also illustrate an ongoing debate over what the Gulag was and what place it should have in public life.

Early Efforts to Remember and Commemorate the Gulag

Early efforts to remember those who suffered and died in the Gulag came even before the collapse of the Soviet Union. Gorbachev's policy of openness (*glasnost*) led to an outpouring of information about the Gulag. Historians gained access to Soviet archives and started reprinting Gulag documents in newspapers, literary magazines, and academic journals. Television programs featured discussions of the Gulag, the Great Terror, and other aspects of Soviet repression. *Cold Summer of 1953*, a 1988 movie about the release of criminals from the Gulag following Stalin's death, was widely viewed by Soviet audiences and won multiple awards. Perhaps most importantly, many former inmates published their memoirs. Aleksandr Solzhenitsyn's famed *Gulag Archipelago*, which appeared in the West in the 1970s, was finally published in his home country in 1990. This in turn prompted ordinary people to try to piece together their own family histories. Nikolai Kovach, for instance, responded to a newspaper advertisement and was reunited with his older sister, from whom he had been separated by the Gulag fifty-four years earlier. Together they then discovered the identities and stories of their parents, causing Nikolai to feel "that he knew who he was now, because he knew who his parents were."[4]

At the same time that efforts were being made to remember the past, Mikhail Gorbachev established a commission to identify victims of Soviet repression and rehabilitate them (i.e., restore legal rights and expunge all record of the alleged crime). Just before the collapse of the Soviet Union, Boris Yeltsin, soon to be president of the Russian Federation, called for another round of case reviews, legal rehabilitation, and compensation for those unjustly punished by Soviet repressive organs. This led to the creation of a special commission that investigated crimes perpetrated by the Soviet state and ultimately granted legal rehabilitation to around 4 million Russian citizens who had served time in the Gulag. Alexander Yakovlev, a prominent ally of Gorbachev and Yeltsin, was central to these legal efforts; he also published widely in Russia and abroad concerning Soviet crimes.

As significant as this public process of legal rehabilitation was, it is striking that a very different type of legal proceeding did not happen: the prosecution of perpetrators. While individual Gulag personnel were occasionally tried and punished for specific crimes, these were selective and secretive processes. No one legally, either during the Khrushchev era of de-Stalinization or in the post-Soviet era, was accused and forced to stand trial for the Gulag as a whole. From the beginning of this process of negotiating Gulag remembrance, it was clear that the state was interested only in identifying victims, not perpetrators. For some, this absence has created a warped memory of the Gulag in which people suffered and died but no one was actually responsible for their trauma; for others, it was the only pragmatic choice. As one Russian expressed after the collapse of the USSR, "Why didn't we put Stalin on trial? … In order to condemn Stalin you'd have to condemn your friends and relatives along with him."[5] There were simply too many people complicit in the totalitarian system of repression, many thought, for legal reckoning against perpetrators to take place.[6]

An important player in constructing the memory of the Gulag and pushing for the legal rehabilitation of victims was the Memorial Society, founded in 1987. The central purpose of Memorial was to "prevent a return to totalitarianism" by promoting "the truth about the historical past and perpetuate the memory of victims of political repression."[7] In a country where non-governmental organizations had been absent for several decades, Memorial established an unwavering position as a defender of the people against government repression, whether past or present.[8] The Memorial Society quickly opened branches with libraries and archives across the Soviet and then post-Soviet space. Activists compiled lists of names of those repressed, published articles about Soviet repression, organized conferences, and participated in local educational programming to instill in the younger generations a memory of Soviet atrocities. Memorial also helped organize commemorative events, such as the Days of Remembrance, held on the Solovetsky Islands in 1989. Yet, even with Gorbachev's policy of openness that was then broadened under Boris Yeltsin, groups such as the Memorial Society had to remain somewhat cautious in their approach to Soviet memory. Many, especially in the state apparatus, still wanted to preserve a sanitized version of Soviet history or else forget it altogether as the country transitioned to democratic capitalism.[9]

A central part of Memorial's mission was contacting former inmates and asking them to submit documents, memoirs, photographs, and artifacts from their period of incarceration. Thousands responded to this call and their formerly private memories and archives became publicly available in Memorial branches across the post-Soviet space. For activists and former inmates alike (and these two groups often overlapped), these artifacts and memories served as evidence against the Soviet regime, if not judicially then at least in the realm of public opinion.[10] As one survivor related, "I wrote my memoirs with the understanding that I had a civic duty to establish at least an outline of what I had experienced and survived …. I was determined to write the pure truth and genuine feelings of people whose fate was the same as mine and to spite our dreadful misfortune."[11] Another felt a "duty to leave my descendants the story of my generation, not in theory, but as it was in real life."[12]

But motives for recording Gulag memoirs varied, as did the narratives constructed by survivors. Some wrote as a form of creative self-expression, while others wrote out of explicitly political or nationalist motives. In this way Memorial created not one story of the Gulag, but thousands. And it is notable that while many Gulag survivors have shared their stories, either in published form or as unpublished memoirs in the local branches of Memorial, many others have kept these traumatic experiences private. Part of this reticence is tied to Soviet prohibitions on discussing the Gulag. The long-enforced silence forced survivors to process their experiences silently and to find various non-public ways of remembering their Gulag experience. These include naming children and pets after significant people from their Gulag past or caring for people associated, however loosely, with their Gulag experience.[13] But many simply endured a painful inability to make sense of their traumatic ordeals and died without leaving their memoirs or other artifacts for posterity.

In addition to this creation of "soft memory" through memory collection, the Memorial Society, along with other state and non-state actors, began to erect sites of "hard memory" dedicated to the victims of the Gulag. On October 30, 1990, more than a year before the collapse of the USSR, the Moscow City Council and Memorial Society jointly erected the first official monument to Gulag victims: a large stone brought from the Solovetsky Island that was placed prominently in front of secret police headquarters, a building where many were imprisoned and tortured during the Great Terror [Figure 6.1]. This date—October 30—was then officially named the Day of Remembrance of the Victims of Political Repressions and it continues to be observed to the present day, with commemorative ceremonies that include solemn readings of the names of victims.

Figure 6.1 The Solovetsky Stone in front of secret police headquarters, Moscow.

Numerous additional monuments and museums soon followed. A similar stone from the Solovetsky Island, adorned with a plaque that reads "To the Prisoners of the Gulag," was placed in Saint Petersburg. The enormous Mask of Sorrows monument, designed by famed sculptor Ernst Neizvestny, was erected on a hill overlooking Magadan, the "capital of the Gulag," in 1996 [Figure 6.2]. Various monuments to those who suffered and died in the Gulag were erected in Norilsk through a joint effort of the regional government and non-governmental organizations. Local authorities opened a museum in the former secret police headquarters in the city of Tomsk. One of the largest and best known of these early sites of "hard memory" was the Memorial Complex of Political Repression, a museum located on the abandoned remains of correctional-labor colony Perm-36, where political prisoners were concentrated from 1972 to 1988. It was run by local activists and, though quite remote, welcomed tens of thousands of visitors each year to see how Soviet prisoners had lived and labored

Figure 6.2 Mask of Sorrows, Magadan.

while the state attempted to "correct" them. It also promoted civil rights in contemporary Russia by convening annual conventions attended by various activists and non-governmental organizations.

These museums and monuments of the 1990s were erected by a variety of individuals, local organizations, and state actors. As such, there was no central message about how to remember the Gulag and commemorate the victims of Soviet violence. Rather, these local organizations and groups of people often argued among themselves as to how and what to commemorate. Ukrainians, Poles, Muslims, and Jews aimed to present a story of how their own people were targeted and suffered, with each using their own symbols and traditions as reference points.[14] In similar fashion, the Russian Orthodox Church erected memorial crosses and chapels on sites of mass burial, regardless of the religious affiliation of those buried. The Memorial Society, by contrast, used in its monuments secular symbols or else religious imagery representing all faith systems, as well as atheism. Thus, whether the Gulag should be remembered primarily as a place of collective human suffering or the suffering of a particular group remained a matter of individual initiative.

Remembering the Gulag under Putin

Since Vladimir Putin's rise to power in 2000, the process of remembering the Gulag has shifted. Russian people increasingly came to associate guilt for the repressive Soviet past with the traumatic loss of empire, economic depression, and the massive crime wave of the 1990s, which were themselves also associated with democracy and Western values. After that calamitous decade, most Russians (to the extent that polling, voting patterns, and sociological research can be believed) wanted to stop being ashamed of their recent history and instead desired to reclaim past imperial glory and move forward triumphantly as a privileged Russian people, distinct in history and values from Western Europe.[15] This mirrors Putin's attitude toward the Soviet, and especially Stalinist, past. He has rehabilitated Stalin's image as a great leader who modernized Russia and defended it against German invasion. And he has talked in glowing terms of many aspects of the Soviet Union, calling its collapse "the greatest geopolitical catastrophe of the century."[16] There is thus broad agreement among the majority of ordinary Russians, along with Putin's dictatorial regime, concerning a triumphant Russian nationalist version of the

Soviet past. And this, one might think, would lead to a desire to simply forget the Gulag, to erase it from the Russian historical consciousness.

Yet this has not happened, at least not fully, in part because the Gulag was so massive in scale that it simply cannot be ignored. It is inscribed in tattoos on the bodies of Russian gangsters. It is still heard in ballads sung by older generations of Russians. It is talked about around kitchen tables. It is found in thousands of published memoirs that are easily accessible in both print and digital format.[17] In regions dominated by the indigenous peoples of Siberia, the tangible memory of the Gulag lives on through intermarriages between former prisoners and natives along with their bi-racial children. In the supernatural realm, the Eveny people who inhabit former camp sites have shared numerous stories of Gulag victims appearing as ghosts, with some abandoning houses inhabited by such apparitions.[18] Such was its scale, deadliness, and longevity that the Gulag simply cannot be forgotten. The problem lingering from the 1990s, then, if forgetting was impossible, was how to think about or represent this seminal institution of Soviet repression.

For its part, the Russian government under Putin has done more than one might think to acknowledge the bloody Soviet past. Putin has strongly condemned Stalin's crimes and the suffering of millions of people in the Gulag. State archives helped publish a series of books and document collections devoted to the Gulag and other forms of Soviet repression. Government-controlled media outlets produced movies and television shows about the Gulag, such as *A.L.Zh.I.R.* (2019), an eleven-part series about a Gulag camp for wives of "traitors of the motherland" that premiered on the television channel NTV (controlled by the state-owned gas monopoly, Gazprom, and widely seen as a mouthpiece for the regime). Putin himself has praised Solzhenitsyn's *Gulag Archipelago* and made it mandatory reading in Russian high schools (it helped that Solzhenitsyn was devoutly Orthodox and a staunch Russian nationalist). And the State Museum of Gulag History (to be discussed shortly) in 2019 published a collection of graphic novels titled *You Are Living*, which depict the experiences of four inmates as they navigate the violent and dehumanizing world of the Stalin-era camps. The novels are intended to enable people "to feel the pain and horror of those unjust times, so that everyone could see how important it is to prevent this from happening again."[19]

So the Gulag is clearly not something that the Putin regime is trying to completely ignore. Moreover, there is not always a consistent message propagated by the state as to how people should think about the Gulag. Even in a dictatorial state like Putin's Russia, memory is a messy and sometimes conflicting process. Still, a few key themes stand out within the broader context of Putin's intensely patriotic nation-building project. First, what we might term a "patriotic memory" of the Gulag focuses on victims rather than perpetrators; the culpable are rarely identified, much less vilified. Second, it is limited in scope, restricted almost exclusively to the Stalin era rather than the Soviet period generally. Third, it often focuses on "silver linings," showing that good things were accomplished at both the individual and societal level even during periods of trauma. Fourth, it tends to be didactic, suggesting that the Russian nation can learn from the past and move forward to a brighter, trauma-free future. In this vein, Putin's government in 2015 issued an official state policy on "the memory of victims of political repressions" that called for the state to work with civil society groups and religious organizations to "strengthen the moral health of Russian society."[20] Under Putin, then, remembering Stalin's crimes was intended to be a top-down process of narrative creation that ultimately drew Russians together as they forged a new destiny with Putin at their helm. In these ways, patriotic remembering of the Gulag tends to promote not a forgetting but a "casual acceptance" of past repression.[21]

The shift from the varied monuments of the 1990s to more patriotic monuments under Putin is exemplified by prominent Gulag museums in Moscow and Perm Province. For over a decade after the collapse of the Soviet Union there was no museum devoted to the Gulag in Moscow. That changed in 2004 when former inmate and historian Anton Antonov-Ovseenko opened, with some funding from the Moscow city government, a small museum on a prominent street close to Red Square. Its collections focused on Stalin's crimes and the suffering of victims, with one area of the museum containing wax figures being tortured. Still, for some the museum presented a fairly patriotic picture of the Soviet Union, with Stalinist terror presented as an aberration, as opposed to exhibitions at the Memorial Society and Sakharov Center that criticized the Soviet project more generally.[22] Ultimately, the Putin regime did little more than ignore the museum for several years until finally deciding to relocate it farther away from the Kremlin in order to repurpose the valuable real estate on which it stood.

The new State Museum of Gulag History, which opened in 2015, is much larger, better funded, and more professional than its predecessor. But it is also further from the Kremlin, tucked invisibly away on a quiet residential street. With significant financial support from both government and civil society and with a director and staff comprised of museum professionals, its message is a bit contested, but the overall effect is essentially patriotic. No perpetrators beyond Stalin and his henchmen are named. The timeframe is restricted to the Stalin era and primarily to the Great Terror. And the end of the museum features newsreel clips of Putin, other state officials, Russian Orthodox clerics, and journalists all talking about how the past must never be forgotten and how the Russian nation, under the present political regime, must come together to prevent such a recurrence. Ultimately, in this presentation, "the state emerges penitently triumphal over its bloody past."[23]

The shift to a patriotic version of Gulag remembrance is also present at the Perm-36 museum, which in the mid-2010s was seized by the regional government. This occurred after a group of self-styled patriotic activists waged a multiyear smear campaign to paint the museum as an anti-Russian institution that foreign governments were using to "brainwash our citizens."[24] Among the more prominent accusations was that the museum portrayed Ukrainian nationalists held at Perm-36 in a positive light, a poignant critique in 2014 as Russia forcibly annexed Crimea and fomented civil war in Eastern Ukraine in the wake of the Maidan Uprising. With Ukrainian nationalists being portrayed as fascists and neo-Nazis by the Putin regime, continuing to honor them in a regional museum was viewed as unforgivable.[25]

After the takeover of Perm-36, the new state-appointed museum director quickly shut down a number of activities, such as an annual forum that attracted academics, artists, and human rights activists. In this way, "liberal" interpretations of the memory site were denied their traditional venue, with the new director ensuring that the repressive past would not be connected to Putin's new brand of authoritarianism.[26] The new director also moved to restructure the museum's exhibits to show how the penal colony contributed to Soviet victory in the Second World War, how exceptional members of the Russian nation served there, and how living conditions steadily improved over time. An exhibit devoted to political and Ukrainian nationalist prisoners, meanwhile, was removed. Thus, although it continued to be commemorated as a site of unjust suffering, Perm-36 was also remembered as a place of Russian nationalist heroism where guards and inmates alike fought for victory over Nazi Germany and then marched steadily toward a more humane era of corrections. It also became, in repressing the memory of Ukrainian nationalism at the very moment when Russia was annexing Crimea, a site of post-Soviet Russian imperialism.[27]

More recently, as the opening paragraph of this book's introduction explained, a large monument to the victims of Soviet repression called the Wall of Grief was erected in 2017 at a prominent intersection in Moscow. Located on Sakharov Street (named after the famous nuclear physicist turned dissident who spent many years in internal exile), it is fairly massive at 6-meters high and 32-meters long, with several large stelae standing in front of it. The wall is made up of half-formed human figures, with human-sized cutouts to allow visitors to imagine themselves as part of this repressed mass of humanity. A plaque indicates that it was erected by order of President Putin using both government funding and contributions from the people. Many viewed this design as a compromise choice selected by a jury comprised of state officials, the director of the State Museum of Gulag History, a representative from the Memorial Society, and other specialists.[28] It provides a space for mourning and reflection without identifying perpetrators or trying to craft a particular narrative. As Putin expressed at the monument's dedication, in a speech that conspicuously never mentioned Stalin by name, "now it is important for all of us to build on the values of trust and stability. Only on this basis will we be able to achieve the goals of our society and our country."[29]

A number of monuments to Soviet repression have also been erected in collaboration with the Russian Orthodox Church, the *de facto* state church under Putin. Most prominently, the Church has constructed a large memorial complex at the Butovo execution site on the outskirts of Moscow, where over 20,000 people were killed during the Great Terror. Chapels, crosses (including one brought from the Solovetsky Islands), and monuments dot the site, which is dedicated to the "new martyrs," Church officials who suffered and died at the hands of Soviet agents. Frescoes on the ceiling of the most prominent chapel even depict believers being gunned down by Soviet policemen. In a visit to the site, Putin, a former secret policeman himself, noted that those killed were "the pride of the nation," thus making the patriotic link between the Russian nation and Russian Orthodoxy explicit.[30] Troubling in this context is the fact that although the vast majority of victims killed at this site were not Orthodox clergy, their lives and deaths are barely mentioned.[31]

The Orthodox Church, with the state's blessing, has constructed numerous other monuments across Russia. In the Siberian town of Lozhok, a chapel dedicated to the new martyrs has been erected on the site of a spring, where supposedly forty clergymen were killed in a Gulag camp that formerly existed there. The city of Omsk has a similar chapel on a spring located on the territory of a former Gulag camp, and both are considered holy sites of local pilgrimage. Beyond monuments, in 2013 the Orthodox Church collaborated with the state to produce "Historical Park Russia—My History," a well-attended multimedia exhibition detailing Russian history from the prehistoric to the present. Not surprisingly, in this exhibition "repressions have been positioned outside the main historical narrative," and when they are broached "it is the memory of the ultimate sacrifice made by the New Martyrs, rather than [the] fate of the ordinary victims" that is highlighted.[32] Such focus on Christian martyrdom constructs a simple but effective narrative of the Gulag that protects believers from issues of past complicity while confirming the post-Soviet religious nationalism espoused by Putin.[33]

Not all monuments erected to commemorate Gulag victims have the explicit blessing, and carefully constructed narrative, of the state.

Most prominently, the Last Address project since 2014 has erected over 1,000 tiny plaques on the houses of victims of Soviet terror, denoting the last place that person lived before arrest. Each plaque bears their name, profession, birth date, arrest date, death date, and rehabilitation date (if applicable). They also feature a small square hole where a picture could have gone, representing the absence of the victim. If the Wall of Sorrow is large and central, calling on the Russian nation to unite, then the Last Address plaques are small and decentralized, with no message other than to remember and mourn. This has provoked anger from Russian nationalists who argue that erecting such plaques "is a dangerous distraction from the task of strengthening our homeland."[34] And while the Last Address Project continues to operate as of this writing in late 2022, its future existence is far from certain.

Looking Forward

In December 2021, the increasingly nationalist and authoritarian Russian state made a new foray in the politics of memory when it successfully prosecuted and forced the closure of the Memorial Society, which has been so pivotal in preserving the memory of the Gulag. In 2014, Memorial was officially designated a "foreign agent" under a new law mandating that all non-governmental organizations that received foreign funding be so labelled. The linguistic association with espionage and treason from the Soviet era was intentional, suggesting to the Russian public that the Memorial Society was harming Russia through its Western money and values. An expanded version of this law was then used to close Memorial, ostensibly for failing to include specific "foreign agent" language in all communications, including social media posts, and for supporting "extremism" and "terrorism." Here too the linguistic parallels to the Great Terror of the 1930s were unmistakable.

The barely concealed reason for closing Memorial was connected to the memory of victims of Soviet oppression. As one Russian analyst remarked, "Memorial has become the primary opponent of the official position on history. The authorities imagine that if you destroy that organization, you can destroy its narrative too." Indeed, this viewpoint was unapologetically confirmed by the state-appointed prosecutor, who argued in court, "Why do we, the offspring of victors, have to repent and be embarrassed, instead of being proud of our glorious past?"[35] Positioning the Russian nation as comprised of morally superior victors, Putin's legal apparatus thus excuses all repressive actions, whether past or present. It creates a memory of the past where Gulag inmates either deserved to suffer or die or else they simply do not deserve to be remembered. Notably, the closure of Memorial occurred as Putin prepared for his 2022 invasion of Ukraine: he clearly wanted Memorial silenced before committing grave crimes against humanity that Memorial would have strongly condemned.

Despite the closure of Memorial, the Gulag legacy in post-Soviet Russia is still alive and very much contested. It endures in movies, memoirs, poetry, and other literature, as well as in the supernatural understanding of Siberia. It lives on in songs and tattoos, particularly in the criminal underworld. It exists in numerous monuments and museums across the post-Soviet space, tangible reminders of past repression and mass incarceration. And for the post-Soviet penal system, the Gulag's legacy means that its operations and reforms are inevitably compared to its Soviet predecessor, despite official protestations. In 2021, for instance, the Russian Federal Service for the Discharge of Punishments announced a plan to put inmates to work on the Baikal-Amur Mainline (BAM), a railroad project through Siberia that Gulag inmates labored on starting in the 1930s. In response to immediate criticism that this appeared to be a restoration of the Gulag, the head of the penal service indignantly retorted, "This will not be the GULAG, this will be absolutely new, respectable conditions."[36] Given the repressive nature of the Putin regime, which is currently (as of this writing in 2022) imprisoning those who publicly oppose the war in Ukraine, such comparisons are not likely to disappear anytime soon.

NOTES

Introduction

1. Neil MacFarquhar, "Critics Scoff as Kremlin Erects Monument to the Repressed," *New York Times*, October 31, 2017; Vera Tolz and Precious N. Chatterje-Doody, "Why Did Putin Build a Monument to Victims of Soviet Repression?" *Washington Post*, November 27, 2017.

2. Robyn Dixon, "Russian Court Abolishes Country's Most Prominent Human Rights Group, Memorial," *Washington Post*, December 28, 2021.

3. Aleksandr Isaevich Solzhenitsyn, *The Gulag Archipelago: An Experiment in Literary Investigation*, 3 vols., trans. Thomas P. Whitney (New York: Harper & Row, 1974–78).

4. Kate Brown, "Out of Solitary Confinement: The History of the Gulag," *Kritika* 8, no. 1 (2007), 67–103; Oleg Khlevniuk, "The Gulag and the Non-Gulag as One Interrelated Whole," in *The Soviet Gulag: Evidence, Interpretation, and Comparison*, ed. Michael David-Fox (Pittsburgh: University of Pittsburgh Press, 2016), 25–41.

5. Clare Anderson, ed., *A Global History of Convicts and Penal Colonies* (London: Bloomsbury Academic, 2018).

6. Daniel Beer, *House of the Dead: Siberian Exile under the Tsars* (New York: Alfred A. Knopf, 2017), 15.

7. Sarah Badcock, *A Prison without Walls? Eastern Siberian Exile in the Last Years of Tsarism* (Oxford: Oxford University Press, 2016).

8. Matthew Stibbe, *Civilian Internment during the First World War: A European and Global History, 1914–1920* (London: Palgrave Macmillan, 2019), 36.

9. Norval Morris and David J. Rothman, eds., *The Oxford History of the Prison: The Practice of Punishment in Western Society* (New York: Oxford University Press, 1998).

10. Bruce F. Adams, *The Politics of Punishment: Prison Reform in Russia, 1863–1917* (DeKalb: Northern Illinois University Press, 1996), 155–6.

11. Adams, *Politics of Punishment*, 192.

12. Andrea Pitzer, *One Long Night: A Global History of Concentration Camps* (New York: Little, Brown and Company, 2017).

13. Stibbe, *Civilian Internment*, 1, 243–44.

Chapter 1

1. Solzhenitsyn, *Gulag Archipelago*, 1:24.

2. Solzhenitsyn, *Gulag Archipelago*, 1:92.

3. Tsuyoshi Hasegawa, *Crime and Punishment in the Russian Revolution: Mob Justice and Police in Petrograd* (London: Belknap, 2017).

4. Michael Jakobson, *Origins of the Gulag: The Soviet Prison Camp System, 1917–1934* (Lexington: University Press of Kentucky, 1993), 25.

5. Jakobson, *Origins of the Gulag*, 10; Galina Mikhailovna Ivanova, *Labor Camp Socialism: The Gulag in the Soviet Totalitarian System*, trans. Carol Flath (Armonk, NY: M. E. Sharpe, 2000), 10.

6. Jakobson, *Origins of the Gulag*, 16.

7. Jakobson, *Origins of the Gulag*, 24.

8. 2 Thess. 3:10 (New King James Version).

9. Ivanova, *Labor Camp Socialism*, 15.

10. Ivanova, *Labor Camp Socialism*, 16.

11. Jakobson, *Origins of the Gulag*, 42.

12. Bertha Babina-Nevskaya, "My First Prison, February 1922," in *Till My Tale Is Told: Women's Memoirs of the Gulag*, ed. Simeon Vilensky (Bloomington: Indiana University Press, 1999), 108.

13. Anne Hartmann, "Concepts of the Criminal in the Discourse of 'Perekovka,'" in *Born to Be Criminal: The Discourse on Criminality and the Practice of Punishment in Late Imperial Russia and Early Soviet Union*, ed. Riccardo Nicolosi and Anne Hartmann (Bielefeld: Transcript, 2017), 175–6.

14. Jakobson, *Origins of the Gulag*, 84.

15. Peter H. Solomon Jr., "Soviet Penal Policy," *Slavic Review* 39, no. 2 (1980), 198.

16. Jakobson, *Origins of the Gulag*, 80.

17. Diane P. Koenker and Ronald D. Bachman, eds., *Revelations from the Russian Archives: Documents in English Translation* (Washington, DC: Library of Congress, 1997), 142.

18. Anne Applebaum, *Gulag: A History* (New York: Doubleday, 2003), 20.

19. Maria Galmarini, "Defending the Rights of Gulag Prisoners: The Story of the Political Red Cross, 1918–38," *Russian Review* 71, no. 1 (2012), 6–29.

20. Andrea Gullota, *Intellectual Life and Literature at Solovki 1923–1930: The Paris of the Northern Concentration Camps* (Oxford: Legenda, 2018), 149.

21. Roy R. Robson, *Solovki: The Story of Russia Told through Its Most Remarkable Island* (New Haven, CT: Yale University Press, 2004), 214.

22. Koenker and Bachman, *Revelations*, 147.

23. Natalia Kuziakina, *Theatre in the Solovki Prison Camp*, trans. Boris M. Meerovich (Luxembourg: Harwood Academic, 1995), 58.

24. Jeffrey Hardy, "Religious Identity, Practice, and Hierarchy at the Solovetskii Camp of Forced Labor of Special Significance," in *Rethinking the Gulag: Sources, Identities, Legacies*, ed. Alan Barenberg and Emily D. Johnson (Bloomington: Indiana University Press, 2022), 27.

25. Gullota, *Intellectual Life and Literature at Solovki*, 7.

26. Mark Vincent, "Us and Them: Criminality and Prisoner Hierarchies in the Early Gulag Press, 1923–1930," *Revolutionary Russia* 32, no. 2 (2019), 279.

27. Vincent, "Us and Them," 281.

Chapter 2

1. Applebaum, *Gulag*, 49.

2. Oleg Khlevniuk, *The History of the Gulag: From Collectivization to the Great Terror*, trans. Vadim A. Staklo (New Haven, CT: Yale University Press, 2004), 9.

3. Cynthia A. Ruder, *Making History for Stalin: The Story of the Belomor Canal* (Gainesville: University Press of Florida, 1998), 147.

4. Maxim Gorky, L. Auerbach, and S. G. Firin, eds., *Belomor: An Account of the Construction of the New Canal between the White Sea and the Baltic Sea* (New York: Harrison Smith and Robert Haas, 1935), 337.

5. Dariusz Tolczyk, *See No Evil: Literary Cover-Ups and Discoveries of the Soviet Camp Experience* (New Haven, CT: Yale University Press, 1999).

6. Khlevniuk, *History of the Gulag*, 334.

7. Khlevniuk, *History of the Gulag*, 24.

8. Steven Barnes, *Death and Redemption: The Gulag and the Shaping of Soviet Society* (Princeton, NJ: Princeton University Press, 2011), 33.

9. Barnes, *Death and Redemption*, 37.

10. Fyodor Vasilcvich Mochulsky, *Gulag Boss: A Soviet Memoir*, trans. Deborah Kaple (Oxford: Oxford University Press, 2010), 33.

11. Lev Razgon, "Jailers," in *Gulag Voices: An Anthology*, ed. Anne Applebaum (New Haven, CT: Yale University Press, 2011), 162.

12. Alan Barenberg, *Gulag Town, Company Town: Forced Labor and Its Legacy in Vorkuta* (New Haven, CT: Yale University Press, 2014), 40–1.

13. Andrei Sokolov, "Forced Labor in Soviet Industry: The End of the 1930s to the Mid-1950s," in *The Economics of Forced Labor*, ed. Paul R. Gregory and Valery Lazarev (Stanford, CA: Hoover Institution Press, 2003), 41.

14. Asif Siddiqi, "Scientists and Specialists in the Gulag: Life and Death in Stalin's 'Sharashka,'" *Kritika* 16, no. 3 (2015), 576.

15. Stephen Kotkin, *Magnetic Mountain: Stalinism as a Civilization* (Berkeley: University of California Press, 1995), 231.

16. Jakobson, *Origins of the Gulag*, 98.

17. Khlevniuk, *History of the Gulag*, 85.

18. Lynne Viola, *The Unknown Gulag: The Lost World of Stalin's Special Settlements* (Oxford: Oxford University Press, 2007), 57.

19. Sira Stepanovna Balashina, "A Life in the Forest," in *Gulag Voices: Oral Histories of Soviet Incarceration and Exile*, ed. Jehanne M. Gheith and Katherine R. Jolluck (New York: Palgrave Macmillan, 2011), 22.

20. Viola, *The Unknown Gulag*, 91.

21. Nicolas Werth, *Cannibal Island: Death in a Siberian Gulag*, trans. Steven Rendall (Princeton, NJ: Princeton University Press, 2007), 180.

22. Terry Martin, "The Origins of Soviet Ethnic Cleansing," *Journal of Modern History* 70, no. 4 (1998), 843.

23. Jon K. Chang, *Burnt by the Sun: The Koreans of the Russian Far East* (Honolulu: University of Hawai'i Press, 2016), 157.

24. Khlevniuk, *History of the Gulag*, 171.

25. Applebaum, *Gulag*, 96.

26. Khlevniuk, *History of the Gulag*, 173–5.

27. Barenberg, *Gulag Town*, 29.

28. Wilson Bell, *Stalin's Gulag at War: Forced Labour, Mass Death, and Soviet Victory in the Second World War* (Toronto: University of Toronto Press, 2018), 41.

29. Barnes, *Death and Redemption*, 2.

Chapter 3

1. Gresham Sykes, *The Society of Captives: A Study of a Maximum Security Prison* (Princeton, NJ: Princeton University Press, 1958), 63–78.

2. Jacques Rossi and Michele Sarde, *Jacques the Frenchman: Memories of the Gulag*, trans. Kersti Colombant (Toronto: University of Toronto Press, 2020), 107.

3. Applebaum, *Gulag*, 172.

4. Oksana Kis, *Survival as Victory: Ukrainian Women in the Gulag*, trans. Lidia Wolanskyj (Cambridge: Harvard Ukrainian Research Institute, 2021), 106.

5. Ivan Chistyakov, *The Day Will Pass Away: The Diary of a Gulag Prison Guard 1935–1936*, trans. Arch Tait (New York: Pegasus Books, 2017), 10.

6. Applebaum, *Gulag*, 191.

7. Solzhenitsyn, *Gulag Archipelago*, 2:415.

8. Solzhenitsyn, *Gulag Archipelago*, 2:198.

9. Solzhenitsyn, *Gulag Archipelago*, 2:594.

10. Leonid Borodkin and Simon Ertz, "Coercion Versus Motivation: Forced Labor in Norilsk," in *The Economics of Forced Labor*, 88.

11. Applebaum, *Gulag*, 223.

12. Eugenia Semyonovna Ginzburg, *Journey into the Whirlwind*, trans. Paul Stevenson and Max Hayward (New York: Harcourt, 1967), 405.

13. Mochulsky, *Gulag Boss*, 35.

14. Barnes, *Death and Redemption*, 41.

15. Ginzburg, *Journey into the Whirlwind*, 406.

16. Khlevniuk, *History of the Gulag*, 76.

17. Golfo Alexopoulos, *Illness and Inhumanity in Stalin's Gulag* (New Haven, CT: Yale University Press, 2017), 25–6.

18. Applebaum, *Gulag*, 221.

19. Kis, *Survival as Victory*, 331.

20. Lev Razgon, "Jailers," in *Gulag Voices: An Anthology*, 145.

21. Khlevniuk, *History of the Gulag*, 229–31.

22. Feliks Arkadievich Serebov, "Bridging Separate Worlds," in *Gulag Voices: Oral Histories*, 178.

23. Chistyakov, *The Day Will Pass Away*, 25.

24. Varlam Shalamov, *Kolyma Tales*, trans. John Glad (London: Penguin, 1995), 204–05.

25. Kis, *Survival as Victory*, 132.

26. Ginzburg, *Journey into the Whirlwind*, 197.

27. Ginzburg, *Journey into the Whirlwind*, 407.

28. Kis, *Survival as Victory*, 145.

29. Anatoly Zhigulin, "On Work," in *Gulag Voices: An Anthology*, 63.

30. Dan Healey, "Lives in the Balance: Weak and Disabled Prisoners and the Biopolitics of the Gulag," in *The Soviet Gulag*, 66.

31. Zhigulin, "On Work," 60.

32. Healey, "Lives in the Balance," 83.

33. Zhigulin, "On Work," 66.

34. Sergei Dovlatov, *The Zone: A Prison Camp Guard's Story*, trans. Anne Frydman (New York: Alfred A. Knopf, 1985), 91.

35. Kis, *Survival as Victory*, 108–09.

36. Jeffrey S. Hardy, "Of Pelicans and Prisoners: Avian-Human Interactions in the Soviet Gulag," *Canadian Slavonic Papers* 60, no. 3–4 (2018), 378.

37. Arsenii Formakov, *Gulag Letters*, ed. and trans. Emily D. Johnson (New Haven, CT: Yale University Press, 2017), 122.

38. Menachem Begin, *White Nights: The Story of a Prisoner in Russia*, trans. Katie Kaplan (New York: Harper & Row, 1979) 157.

39. Ginzburg, *Journey into the Whirlwind*, 412–14.

40. Steven Maddox, "Gulag Football: Competitive and Recreational Sport in Stalin's System of Forced Labor," *Kritika: Explorations in Russian and Eurasian History* 19, no. 3 (2018), 535.

41. Kazimierz Zarod, "A Day in Labor Corrective Camp No. 21," in *Gulag Voices: An Anthology*, 54.

42. Inna Klause, "Music and 'Re-Education' in the Soviet Gulag," *Torture Journal* 23, no. 2 (2013), 31.

43. Alexander Dolgun, *Alexander Dolgun's Story* (New York: Alfred A. Knopf, 1975), 226.

44. Barenberg, *Gulag Town*, 70–1.

45. Formakov, *Gulag Letters*, 58.

46. Kis, *Survival as Victory*, 362.

47. Kis, *Survival as Victory*, 365.

48. Janusz Bardach, *Man Is Wolf to Man: Surviving the Gulag*, trans. Kathleen Gleeson (Berkeley: University of California Press, 1998), 208.

49. Hava Volovich, "My Child," in *Gulag Voices: An Anthology*, 98.

50. Wilson Bell, "Sex, Pregnancy, and Power in the Late Stalinist Gulag," *Journal of the History of Sexuality* 24, no. 2 (2015), 198–224; Dan Healy, *Russian Homophobia from Stalin to Sochi* (London: Bloomsbury, 2017), 27–40.

51. Volovich, "My Child," 99.

52. Elaine McKinnon, "Motherhood and Survival in the Stalinist Gulag," *Aspasia* 13 (2019), 65–94.

Chapter 4

1. Solzhenitsyn, *Gulag Archipelago*, 3:9–10.

2. Edwin Bacon, *The Gulag at War: Stalin's Forced Labour System in Light of the Archives* (New York: New York University Press, 1994), 137.

3. Mochulsky, *Gulag Boss*, 98–9.

4. Barnes, *Death and Redemption*, 131.

5. Razgon, "Jailers," 158.

6. Alexopoulos, *Illness and Inhumanity*, 140–59; Mikhail Nakonechnyi, "'They Won't Survive for Long,'" in *Rethinking the Gulag*, 103–28.

7. Bell, *Stalin's Gulag at War*, 74.

8. Pavel Polian, *Against Their Will: The History and Geography of Forced Migrations in the USSR* (Budapest: Central European University Press, 2004).

9. J. Otto Pohl, "A Caste of Helot Labourers: Special Settlers and the Cultivation of Cotton in Soviet Central Asia: 1944–1956," in *The Cotton Sector in Central Asia: Economic Policy and Development Challenges*, ed. Deniz Kandiyoti (London: University of London, 2007), 28.

10. Anna Cieślikowska, "Fragments," in *Gulag Voices: Oral Histories*, 203.

11. Adam Jones, *Genocide: A Comprehensive Introduction*, 3rd ed. (London: Routledge, 2017), 18.

12. Norman M. Naimark, *Stalin's Genocides* (Princeton, NJ: Princeton University Press, 2010), 135.

13. Francine Hirsch, *Soviet Judgment at Nuremburg: A New International History of the International Military Tribunal after World War II* (New York: Oxford University Press, 2020), 235.

14. Klaus Mülhahn, "'Repaying Blood Debt,'" in *The Soviet Gulag*, 264.

15. Harry Wu and Carolyn Wakeman, *Bitter Winds: A Memoir of My Years in China's Gulag* (New York: John Wiley & Sons, 1994), 123.

16. Ulrich Merten, *The Gulag in East Germany: Soviet Special Camps, 1945–1950* (Amherst, NY: Teneo, 2018), 120.

17. István Fehérváry, *The Long Road to Revolution: The Hungarian Gulag, 1945–1956*, trans. Zsuzsa Gorka (Santa Fe, NM: Pro Libertate, 1989), 118.

18. Milada Polišcnská, *Czechoslovak's Diplomacy and the Gulag: Deportation of Czechoslovak Citizens to the USSR and the Negotiation for Their Repatriation, 1945–1953* (Budapest: Central European University Press, 2015), 56.

19. Michael Solomon, *Magadan* (Princeton, NJ: Vertex Books, 1971), 44.

20. Solzhenitsyn, *Gulag Archipelago*, 2:136.

21. Golfo Alexopoulos, "Amnesty 1945: The Revolving Door of Stalin's Gulag," *Slavic Review* 64, no. 2 (2005), 298.

22. Nina Ivanovna Rodina, "It Wasn't Life," in *Gulag Voices: Oral Histories*, 104.

23. Ginzburg, *Journey Into the Whirlwind*, 294.

24. Barnes, *Death and Redemption*, 166.

25. Dolgun, *Alexander Dolgun's Story*, 218.

26. Solomon, *Magadan*, 89.

27. Tomasz Kizny, *Gulag: Life and Death inside the Soviet Concentration Camps* (Buffalo, NY: Firefly Books), 434–93.

28. Barenberg, *Gulag Town*, 94.

29. Solomon, *Magadan*, 118.

30. Kis, *Survival as Victory*, 176.

31. Nina Gagen-Torn, "On Faith," in *Gulag Voices: An Anthology*, 75–6.

32. Solzhenitsyn, *Gulag Archipelago*, 3:100–01.

33. John H. Noble and Glenn D. Everett, *I Found God in Soviet Russia* (New York: St. Martin's Press, 1963), 108, 118–28, 138–46.

34. Kis, *Survival as Victory*, 214.

35. Bardach, *Man Is Wolf to Man*, 221.

36. Mark Vincent, *Criminal Subculture in the Gulag: Prisoner Society in the Stalinist Labour Camps, 1924–53* (London: Bloomsbury Academic, 2020), 162.

37. Mark Galeotti, *The Vory: Russia's Super Mafia* (New Haven: Yale University Press, 2018), 45.

38. Galeotti, *The Vory*, 47.

39. Solomon, *Magadan*, 138–9.

40. Applebaum, *Gulag*, 469.

41. M. Cherif Bassiouni, *Crimes against Humanity: Historical Evolution and Contemporary Application* (Cambridge: Cambridge University Press, 2011), 200.

Chapter 5

1. Paul Gregory, "An Introduction to the Economics of the Gulag," in *The Economics of Forced Labor*, 11–12; Khlevniuk, "The Economy of the OGPU," 55, 64.

2. Barnes, *Death and Redemption*, 203.

3. Ginzburg, *Journey into the Whirlwind*, 359.

4. Khlevniuk, "The Gulag and the Non-Gulag," 41.

5. Solzhenitsyn, *The Gulag Archipelago*, 3:494.

6. Jeffrey S. Hardy, *The Gulag after Stalin: Redefining Punishment in Khrushchev's Soviet Union, 1953–1964* (Ithaca, NY: Cornell University Press, 2016), 204.

7. Solzhenitsyn, *Gulag Archipelago*, 3:303.

8. Applebaum, *Gulag*, 506.

9. Barnes, *Death and Redemption*, 246.

10. Nanci Adler, *The Gulag Survivor: Beyond the Soviet System* (New Brunswick, NJ: Transaction, 2002), 109.

11. Danylo Shumuk, *Life Sentence: Memoirs of a Ukrainian Political Prisoner*, trans. Ivan Jaworsky and Halya Kowalska (Edmonton: Canadian Institute of Ukrainian Studies, University of Alberta, 1984), 308.

12. Barenberg, *Gulag Town*, 200.

13. Barenberg, *Gulag Town*, 206.

14. Nanci Adler, *Keeping Faith with the Party: Communist Believers Return from the Gulag* (Bloomington: Indiana University Press, 2012), 114.

15. Svetlana Alexievich, *Secondhand Time: The Last of the Soviets* (New York: Random House, 2016), 101.

16. Hardy, *Gulag After Stalin*, 72.

17. Miriam Dobson, *Khrushchev's Cold Summer: Gulag Returnees, Crime, and the Fate of Reform after Stalin* (Ithaca, NY: Cornell University Press, 2009), 146–50.

18. Hardy, *Gulag after Stalin*, 19–95; Healy, *Russian Homophobia*, 40–50.

19. Jeffrey Hardy, "Gulag Tourism: Khrushchev's 'Show' Prisons in the Cold War Context, 1954–1959," *Russian Review* 71, no. 1 (2012), 75.

20. Hardy, *Gulag after Stalin*, 76–7.

21. Hardy, *Gulag after Stalin*, 130.

22. Hardy, *Gulag after Stalin*, 75.

23. Anatoly Marchenko, *My Testimony*, trans. Michel Scammell (New York: E. P. Dutton, 1969), 49.

24. Helene Celmina, *Women in Soviet Prisons* (New York: Paragon House, 1985), 131.

25. Hardy, *Gulag after Stalin*, 163.

26. Marc Elie and Jeffrey S. Hardy, "'Letting the Beasts out of the Cage': Parole in the Post-Stalin Gulag, 1953–1973," *Europe-Asia Studies* 67, no. 4 (2015), 579–605.

27. Andrei Amalrik, *Notes of a Revolutionary*, trans. Guy Daniels (New York: Alfred A. Knopf, 1982), 183.

28. Vladimir Bukovsky, *To Build a Castle: My Life as a Dissenter*, trans. Michael Scammell (New York: Viking Press, 1979), 45.

29. Amalrik, *Notes of a Revolutionary*, 222.

30. Bukovsky, *To Build a Castle*, 322.

31. Masha Gessen and Misha Friedman, *Never Remember: Searching for Stalin's Gulags in Putin's Russia* (New York: Columbia Global Reports, 2018), 101.

32. Gessen and Friedman, *Never Remember*, 99.

33. Bukovsky, *To Build a Castle*, 36.

34. Marchenko, *My Testimony*, 355.

35. Amnesty International, *Prisoners of Conscience in the USSR* (London: Amnesty International Publications, 1975), 196.

36. Amnesty International, *Prisoners*, 198.

37. William Pomeranz, *Law and the Russian State: Russia's Legal Evolution from Peter the Great to Vladimir Putin* (London: Bloomsbury, 2019), 109.

38. Jonathan Daly, *Crime and Punishment in Russia: A Comparative History from Peter the Great to Vladimir Putin* (London: Bloomsbury, 2019), 147–8.

39. Jean-Pierre Vaudon, "Last Days of the GULAG?" *National Geographic* 177, no. 3 (1990), 44.

40. Michael Bordeaux, *Gorbachev, Glasnost and the Gospel* (London: Hodder and Stoughton, 1990), 197.

41. Gavin Slade, "'Who Are You in Life?'," in *Rethinking the Gulag*, 77.

42. Khlevniuk, "The Gulag and Non-Gulag," 40–1.

Chapter 6

1. Judith Pallot, Laura Piacentini and Dominique Moran, *Gender, Geography, and Punishment: The Experience of Women in Carceral Russia* (Oxford: Oxford University Press, 2012).

2. Judith Pallot, Laura Piacentini and Dominique Moran, "Patriotic Discourses in Russia's Penal Peripheries: Remembering the Mordovan Gulag," *Europe-Asia Studies* 62, no. 1 (2010), 14.

3. Alexander Etkind, *Warped Mourning: Stories of the Undead in the Land of the Unburied* (Stanford, CA: Stanford University Press, 2013), 177.

4. Gessen and Friedman, *Never Remember*, 45.

5. Alexievich, *Secondhand Time*, 32.

6. Gessen and Friedman, *Never Remember*, 105.

7. *The Charter of the International Volunteer Public Organization "Memorial" Historical, Educational, Human Rights and Charitable Society*, adopted April 19, 1992.

8. Zuzanna Bogumił, *Gulag Memories: The Rediscovery and Commemoration of Russia's Repressive Past* (New York: Berghahn Books, 2022), 46.

9. Kathleen E. Smith, *Remembering Stalin's Victims: Popular Memory and the End of the USSR* (Ithaca, NY: Cornell University Press, 1996), 105–06.

10. Nanci Adler, *Victims of Soviet Terror: The Story of the Memorial Movement* (Westport, CT: Praeger, 1993), 106.

11. Kis, *Survival as Victory*, 74.

12. Kis, *Survival as Victory*, 76.

13. Jehanne Gheith, "'I Never Talked': Enforced Silence, Non-Narrative Memory, and the Gulag," *Mortality* 12, no. 2 (2007), 161.

14. Bogumił, *Gulag Memories*, 67.

15. Bogumił, *Gulag Memories*, 198.

16. Fiona Hill and Clifford G. Gaddy, *Mr. Putin: Operative in the Kremlin* (Washington, DC: Brookings Institution Press, 2015), 56.

17. The largest body of Russian-language digital memoirs—over 1,600 at the time of this writing—is found on the website of the Sakharov Center: https://www.sakharov-center.ru/asfcd/auth/?t=list.

18. Olga Ulturgasheva, "Ghosts of the Gulag in the Eveny World of the Dead," *Polar Journal* 7, no. 1 (2017), 3.

19. The English version of the collection is called *The Survivors*. Museum of Gulag History, "The Survivors," available at https://gmig.ru/en/projects/survivors. Accessed April 6, 2022.

20. Thomas Sniegon, "Dying in the Soviet Gulag for the Future Glory of Mother Russia? Making 'Patriotic' Sense of the Gulag in Present-Day Russia," in *Cultural and Political Imaginaries in Putin's Russia*, ed. Niklas Bernsand and Barbara Törnquist-Plewa (Leiden: Brill, 2018), 105.

21. Nanci Adler and Anton Weiss-Wendt, "Introduction: Revisiting the Future of the Soviet Past and the Memory of Stalinist Repression," in *The Future of the Soviet Past: The Politics of Memory in Putin's Russia*, ed. Anton Weiss-Wendt and Nanci Adler (Bloomington: Indiana University Press, 2021), 1.

22. Sniegon, "Dying in the Soviet Gulag," 127–8.

23. Jeffrey S. Hardy, "Commemorating and Forgetting Soviet Repression: Moscow's State Museum of GULAG History," in *Museums of Communism: New Memory Sites in Central and Eastern Europe* (Bloomington: Indiana University Press, 2020), 295.

24. Steven A. Barnes, "Keeping the Past in the Past: The Attack on the Perm 36 Gulag Museum and Russian Historical Memory of Soviet Repression," in *The Future of the Soviet Past*, 116.

25. J. Paul Goode, "Patriotism without Patriots? Perm'-36 and Patriotic Legitimation in Russia," *Slavic Review* 79, no. 2 (Summer 2020), 402–08.

26. Barnes, "Keeping the Past in the Past," 126.

27. Bogumił, *Gulag Memories*, 142.

28. Kathleen E. Smith, "A Monument for Our Times? Commemorating Victims of Repression in Putin's Russia," *Europe-Asia Studies* 71, no. 8 (2019), 1314.

29. Smith, "A Monument for Our Times," 1338.

30. Sniegon, "Dying in the Soviet Gulag," 121.

31. Julie Fedor and Tomas Sniegon, "The Butovskii Shooting Range," in *Museums of Communism*, 304–43.

32. Bogumił, *Gulag Memories*, 197.

33. Jeanmarie Rouhier-Willoughby, "The Gulag Reclaimed as Sacred Space: The Negotiation of Memory at the Holy Spring of Iskitim," *Laboratorium: Russian Review of Social Research* 7, no. 1 (2015), 68.

34. Marc Bennetts, "A Drive to Remember Stalin's Victims Is Being Threatened by Putin's Push to Revise History," *Newsweek*, September 9, 2015. Available at https://www.newsweek.com/2015/09/18/drive-remember-stalins-victims-being-threatened-putins-push-revise-history-369532.html.

35. Felix Light, "Russian Court Orders Closure of Renowned Rights Group Memorial," *The Moscow Times*, December 28, 2021. Available at https://www.themoscowtimes.com/2021/12/28/russian-court-orders-closure-of-renowned-rights-group-memorial-a75674.

36. Natalya Skorlygina, "Balki pozornye," *Kommersant*, May 26, 2021. Available at https://www.kommersant.ru/doc/4827428.

SELECT BIBLIOGRAPHY

Alexopoulos, Golfo. *Illness and Inhumanity in Stalin's Gulag*. New Haven, CT: Yale University Press, 2017.

Applebaum, Anne. *Gulag: A History*. New York: Doubleday, 2003.

Applebaum, Anne, ed. *Gulag Voices: An Anthology*. New Haven, CT: Yale University Press, 2011.

Barenberg, Alan. *Gulag Town, Company Town: Forced Labor and Its Legacy in Vorkuta*. New Haven, CT: Yale University Press, 2014.

Barenberg, Alan, and Emily D. Johnson, eds. *Rethinking the Gulag: Identities, Sources, Legacies*. Bloomington: Indiana University Press, 2022.

Barnes, Steven. *Death and Redemption: The Gulag and the Shaping of Soviet Society*. Princeton, NJ: Princeton University Press, 2011.

Bell, Wilson. *Stalin's Gulag at War: Forced Labour, Mass Death, and Soviet Victory in the Second World War*. Toronto: University of Toronto Press, 2018.

Bogumił, Zuzanna. *Gulag Memories*. Translated by Philip Palmer. New York: Berghahn Books, 2022.

Daly, Jonathan. *Crime and Punishment in Russia: A Comparative History from Peter the Great to Vladimir Putin*. London: Bloomsbury, 2019.

David-Fox, Michael, ed. *The Soviet Gulag: Evidence, Interpretation, and Comparison*. Pittsburgh, PA: University of Pittsburgh Press, 2016.

Gheith, Jehanne M., and Katherine R. Jolluck, eds. *Gulag Voices: Oral Histories of Soviet Incarceration and Exile*. New York: Palgrave Macmillan, 2011.

Ginzburg, Eugenia Semyonovna. *Journey into the Whirlwind*. Translated by Paul Stevenson and Max Hayward. New York: Harcourt, 1967.

Gregory, Paul R., and Valery Lazarev, eds. *The Economics of Forced Labor*. Stanford, CA: Hoover Institution Press, 2003.

Hardy, Jeffrey S. *The Gulag after Stalin: Redefining Punishment in Khrushchev's Soviet Union, 1953–1964*. Ithaca, NY: Cornell University Press, 2016.

Ivanova, Galina Mikhailovna. *Labor Camp Socialism: The Gulag in the Soviet Totalitarian System*. Translated by Carol Flath. Armonk, NY: M. E. Sharpe, 2000.

Select Bibliography

Jakobson, Michael. *Origins of the Gulag: The Soviet Prison Camp System, 1917–1934*. Lexington: University Press of Kentucky, 1993.

Khlevniuk, Oleg. *The History of the Gulag: From Collectivization to the Great Terror*. Translated by Vadim A. Staklo. New Haven, CT: Yale University Press, 2004.

Kis, Oksana. *Survival as Victory: Ukrainian Women in the Gulag*. Translated by Lidia Wolanskyj. Cambridge: Harvard Ukrainian Research Institute, 2021.

Shalamov, Varlam. *Kolyma Tales*. Translated by John Glad. London: Penguin, 1994.

Solzhenitsyn, Aleksandr Isaevich. *The Gulag Archipelago: An Experiment in Literary Investigation*. 3 vols. Translated by Thomas P. Whitney. New York: Harper & Row, 1974–78.

Vilensky, Simeon, ed. *Till My Tale Is Told: Women's Memoirs of the Gulag*. Bloomington: Indiana University Press, 1999.

Viola, Lynne. *The Unknown Gulag: The Lost World of Stalin's Special Settlements*. Oxford: Oxford University Press, 2007.

INDEX

Index

Index

Index